Edinburgh
2010

YOUTH PERSPECTIVES

Edinburgh 2010

Youth Perspectives

Edited by Kirk Sandvig

WILLIAM CAREY INTERNATIONAL UNIVERSITY PRESS
PASADENA, CALIFORNIA

Edinburgh 2010: Youth Perspectives

Copyright © 2010 by Edinburgh 2010

All rights reserved.

ISBN: 9780865850125

Published by William Carey International University Press
1539 E. Howard Street, Pasadena, California 91104

William Carey International University Press publishes works that further the university's objective to prepare men and women to discover and address the roots of human problems around the world.

Printed in the United States of America.

Contents

Preface

I sometimes tell my students that, whenever my awareness of my advancing years threatens to depress me, I decide to attend a missionary meeting, for I know that I shall come away immensely encouraged by the abundant evidence that I am not so old after all! Enthusiasm for the world mission of the Christian Church appears, in much of the western world, to be the preserve of a diminishing and ageing constituency. At least in Britain, meetings convened for the purpose of enthusing or informing Christians about the Church in the majority world and its mission rarely attract the younger generation, despite the stories of church growth and courageous Christian witness in hostile or difficult environments that such meetings are often able to tell.

It might be tempting to conclude, therefore, that the subjects of mission and youth no longer belong together. This volume of essays commissioned by the Council of the Edinburgh 2010 centenary conference suggests, however, that there is another side to the picture. The ten contributors to this book are all under the age of thirty and yet are all passionately committed to a missional understanding of the Christian faith. They also share a belief that mission is a subject that demands both serious theological reflection and appropriate action characterised, in David J. Bosch's famous phrase, by 'bold humility'. The essays have been selected from the entries to a youth writing competition organised by Kirk Sandvig, the youth co-ordinator of the Edinburgh 2010 project. The range of the essayists reflects the range of the entrants to the competition rather than being fully representative of the distribution of the world Christian family. Entrants from North America predominate, and the continent of Africa, so central in the story of the geographical realignment of Christianity to the southern hemisphere since the middle of the twentieth century, is sadly not represented at all in this collection. This is especially regrettable, not least because it mirrors the serious neglect of Africa by the World Missionary Conference held in Edinburgh in 1910, at which there was only one delegate from black Africa. Happily, the other (and even more gravely) neglected continent at Edinburgh 1910, Latin America, is represented in this collection by the essay from Luiz Coelho from Brazil, in addition to figuring in the text of several of the other essays.

Despite the imbalance in the range of the contributors, the themes with which these essays grapple are those that occur again and again in contemporary debates over Christian mission: the meaning of the Christian missionary imperative in pluralistic religious contexts, the relationship of mission and unity, the missionary calling of the Church amidst injustice and oppression, and the paradigmatic nature of the *missio Dei* for the mission programmes that Christians adopt, are all central to this volume. Andrew Thompson's opening essay in particular engages with the central problem of the uncongenial nature of the 'mission' word to many younger Christians today, or at least with its high embarrassment factor when placed in an intercultural or global context.

Delegates to the World Missionary Conference in 1910 were distinguished by their predominantly grey or white heads, according to one contemporary journalist's report. Yet perhaps the most powerful address given at Edinburgh 1910 was that delivered by one of the youngest participants, Cheng Jingyi, the twenty-eight-year-old assistant pastor from Beijing who confronted the assembly with the challenge that Chinese Christians were calling with some impatience for a non-denominational expression of the faith in their national context. His words had a great impact, and this young Chinese found himself catapulted as a result into a position of leadership in the Continuation Committee and in the history of ecumenical initiatives in Chinese Christianity. It is not too much to hope that the voices of young Christians, eager, as Cheng was, to express the missionary nature of Christianity in ways that make sense to their own generation, will have a similar impact on the centenary conference that gathers in Edinburgh in June 2010.

Brian Stanley
Director, Centre for the Study of World Christianity,
University of Edinburgh,
April 2010

Introduction

Youth perspectives on mission have often been unrecognized during the discussions of Christian witness throughout the world. Most discussions of mission have tended to be dominated by 'more experienced' and 'accomplished' missiologists that we all know and respect. This perceived dominance has, unfortunately, created reluctance among many young missionaries and missiologists to freely express their thoughts on Christian witness. While many people have written *about* the role of youth within the Church, very little has actually been written *from* the perspective of youth. This, however, does not mean that youth have nothing to contribute on the subject of Christian witness in the world today. As we will see in this book, the perspectives of youth provide an invaluable asset to the Church as a whole, and their participation into the discussion of Christian witness is strongly needed.

In an effort to increase youth participation and foster creative thinking within the Edinburgh 2010 process, a youth writing contest was established in order to provide youth an opportunity to share their thoughts on the issues of Christian witness. Youth, ages 18-30, were encouraged to write a 3000-word essay, engaging in one of the nine study themes of the

Edinburgh 2010 conference.

The nine study themes are:
- Foundations for Mission
- Christian Mission Among Other Faiths
- Mission and Post-Modernity
- Mission and Power
- Forms of Missionary Engagement
- Theological Education and Formation
- Christian Communities in Contemporary Contexts
- Mission and Unity—Ecclesiology and Mission
- Mission Spirituality and Authentic Discipleship

After receiving essays from youth spanning around the world, including: South Africa, Nigeria, Kenya, Rwanda, Myanmar, Malaysia, the Philippines, Brazil, the US, Canada, Germany, and the UK, this book will represent the top 10 essays submitted for the contest. An evaluation panel of top missiologists and theologians of various backgrounds have selected the top essays. Through careful consideration, these essays represent a variety of theological, denominational, confessional, and geographical perspectives, as they engage the various study themes. While not all of the study themes have been represented in this book, these essays do represent many of the themes discussed during Edinburgh 2010 conference.

Given the nature of the Edinburgh 2010 conference, the essays selected for this book exhibit many different writing styles. Some of the essays have more of an academic approach to the study themes, while others take on a more personal approach. In either case, the authors of these essays offer new and innovative ways of critically evaluating our approach to Christian witness in twenty-first century.

Special thanks to all the authors who submitted to the Edinburgh 2010 Youth Writing Contest, the Youth Writing

Contest Panel, the Edinburgh 2010 Staff, the World Council of Churches, and all connected to the William Carey International Press for making this publication possible.

Kirk Sandvig
Edinburgh 2010 Youth and Mission Coordinator

1

Communities of the Spirit: The Missiology of Roland Allen in the Twenty-First Century

Christian Communities in Contemporary Contexts

Andrew R. H. Thompson[1]

"I hate it," responded one disaffected seminarian. "I hate the word 'mission.'" The seminarians were preparing for a trip to El Salvador, and were discussing missiology and its various implications. All of the students were ambivalent about the idea of mission, and they reflected on the various possible locutions to describe to others the purpose of their upcoming trip: "service," "volunteer," "study," "relationship-building." Anything but "mission."

These students are not alone in their uncertainty. Conversations like this occur throughout the church, some with reactions every bit as adverse as that of the student above. Church groups on short-term visits wonder what it means to call such a thing "mission." A group of young adults preparing for their departure into the field struggles with the connotations of the term "missionary," most opting for "volunteer," or "community development worker."[2] These conversations reflect an understanding of mission primarily as an encounter between distinct cultures, usually characterized by inequality of wealth or power, and accordingly they express discomfort with the colonialist or imperialistic connotations and history of mission so conceived. Likewise, the choice of labels like "service" points to a recognition that the church must attend to communities' material needs, and a belief (justified or not) that mission may not always include such attention. These sentiments are especially prevalent among young leaders in the church, such as the seminarians and missionaries above, who see mission as a relic of a less pluralist, less culturally aware past, and yet struggle to reconcile this perspective with the mandate to "go and make disciples of all nations" (Matt 28.19).

Such a narrow view of mission, as primarily one-way, from "developed" or "advanced" societies to "developing" or "third-world" countries, with all of its attendant implications, is inadequate to address the contemporary faith of Christians, young and old; it is also theologically impoverished. Yet it persists in the face of decades of efforts to provide more appropriate missiological frameworks.[3] In my own tradition, leaders of the Anglican Communion called upon the church to "rethink the whole idea of mission" in terms that reflect equality, interdependence, and mutual responsibility as early as 1963.[4] Nonetheless, the objections and ambivalence described above suggest a perception that these conceptual changes have not always translated into notable shifts in practice. Appropriately for this centenary, a practical missiology that meets these twenty-first century needs is found in the writings of a missionary from the turn of the previous century, Roland Allen. Allen's challenge to the missionary practices of his time, with their dependence on what he called "the modern Western spirit", and call for greater trust in the work of the Holy Spirit in mission communities, are as relevant to our current situation as they were a century ago.

Before turning to Allen's methods, though, I consider one conception of mission that addresses some of the contemporary concerns already noted. A more theologically appropriate missiology views mission as the concrete witness of Christian communities in all places—"the whole church bringing the whole Gospel to the whole world."[5] The ecclesiology of John Howard Yoder presents a compelling call for just such a view, one that will subsequently be clarified by the methods commended by Roland Allen.

I. PROCLAIMING THE MISSIO DEI

Mission is the concrete witness of Christian communities in the world. Since the middle of the twentieth century Christians have affirmed that Christian mission is always a participation in the *missio Dei*, God's saving purpose for the world.[6] The core of mission, then, must be the faithful witness of Christians to the *missio Dei*, our testimony to God's reconciling purpose for creation that embraces and subsumes and saves all other goals and acts. Mission is therefore central to the identity of the church itself, as the faithful community that exists as a sign, in the world, of God's mission. Conversely, the primary locus of Christian participation in God's mission is the church, or, more specifically, the faithful communities that testify to the *missio Dei*; in other words, the church is central to mission. The "sending" to which the etymology of "mission" refers is not the sending of individuals by one community to another, but rather the sending of God's people by God in witness into the world.

John Howard Yoder's ecclesiology helps clarify the content of this proclamation.[7] He describes the community's mission as a "modeling mission," in that, "the church is called to be now what the world is called to be ultimately."[8] In other words, the example of the church testifies to God's purpose for creation—

the *missio Dei*. Specifically, the witnessing community enacts values of reconciliation, peacefulness, and egalitarianism in the midst of a world that undermines or rejects those values. Because the God it proclaims is other than and beyond the world, the church's ability to carry out this modeling mission depends on its ability to stand against the wisdom and values of the world when necessary.[9] It thereby proclaims by example God's desire for human life in community as revealed by Jesus, and works toward some partial realization of that desire.

The witness of Yoder's Christian community is theologically founded. Its first and core commitment is to Christ's example, most fundamentally His cross. The believers' cross mandated in the New Testament is our imitation of Jesus in his disavowal of worldly ways of relating to others.[10] It is our willing acceptance of rejection and suffering as potential consequences of our testimony. Witnessing to God's mission of reconciliation and peace necessarily places believers apart from—yet always in mission to and in service of, never purely against—the world to which they are sent.

Yet Yoder's vision is also culturally apt: it acknowledges and addresses contemporary concerns about pluralism. He argues that gaps between different cultures or beliefs are not bridged by some universal metalanguage, but rather by our own particular witnesses proclaimed in the language of pluralism.[11] We are called to discern how to proclaim Christ's lordship in a way that is meaningful to a pluralist world, the same way the first Christians discerned how to proclaim it in new and different contexts.[12] Yoder refers to this as a "missionary ethic of incarnation."[13] God became incarnate to call us to a particular way of participating in the *missio Dei*, and we can extend that invitation to all. The fact that the truth has taken on particularity in a particular time and place is the basis for our engagement with other ways of believing.

We proclaim this truth not by seeking to be less specifically Christian, but rather by working at every commonality and conflict to which our particularity leads us. As we shall see, Allen's missionary methods provide some suggestions for our discernment of the shape of this engagement. The existence of Christian communities testifies to the fact that our truth, like all truth, is particular, and precisely in this particularity, it can be meaningfully communicated—universally—to other particular contexts. As Yoder says, "we report an event that occurred in our listeners' own world, and ask them to respond to it. What could be more universal than that?"[14]

II. ROLAND ALLEN: COMMUNITIES OF THE SPIRIT

Roland Allen, an Anglican missionary in China at the turn of the twentieth century, criticizes the missionary practices of that period. His challenges invite comparison with modern concerns and suggest methods for realizing Yoder's notion of a particular communal witness in a pluralist context. Allen argues that the "modern Western spirit," suffers from a lack of trust in the presence of the Holy Spirit in mission communities, creates utter dependence on the missionary, and is inconsistent with the practices modeled by the most successful missionary in the history of the faith, St. Paul, who was able to establish viable Christian communities in four provinces of the Roman Empire in the ten years between 47 and 57 C.E.[15]

Allen elaborates St. Paul's methods, addressing his administration of the communities (including leadership and finances), his preaching, and his use of miracles.[16] First, in contrast to the administrative methods of his modern-day successors, the key to Paul's success is "that he founded churches whilst we found missions."[17] That is, Allen's contemporaries gather dependent communities around a single missionary, usually sent and supported by an elaborate foreign organization, who administers the sacraments and delivers the teachings of the faith. Paul, on the other hand, incorporated the local leadership, introduced the fundamental elements of the Gospel and Old Testament and basic sacraments, and, usually after five or six months, left behind a viable church in the care of local elders.[18] He taught in a context of mutual instruction, allowing "local prophets" to speak, then withdrew from the community to enable local leadership. Of course, Paul maintained communication with the churches through his letters. Nonetheless, according to Allen, Paul consistently emphasized the importance of their freedom.[19] Paul's financial practices also supported this: he did not establish financially dependent communities. Rather, financial matters were always means to strengthen the unity of the Body of Christ.[20]

Allen surveys the accounts of St. Paul's preaching, and discerns a characteristic recognition and understanding of the particular "condition" of his listeners as regards their current beliefs, and a corresponding effort to address their own peculiar challenges to accepting the Gospel.[21] Underlying this approach is a frank acknowledgment of the general difficulty of such acceptance, as well as respect for the hearers' understanding and confidence in the message itself. These aspects portray a style of teaching that gave careful attention to the specific circumstances of the communities. Finally, according to Allen, Paul's working of miracles and teachings on charity (such as 1 Corinthians 13.1-3) illustrate Christian concern for "doing good," a perspective that saw, "in every case of trouble or disease...an opportunity for the revelation of grace and loving-kindness."[22] Miracles and service manifested the Spirit and character of the new religion.

This latter point deserves more consideration than Allen gives it. God's desire for creation is more comprehensive than material well-being; our participation in the *missio Dei* therefore cannot be reduced to social or economic development programs. On the other hand, neither can it ignore the concrete realities of those to whom it is addressed. Indeed, one aspect of modern dissatisfaction with the idea of mission is based on a perception, noted above, that missions have neglected these realities in the past. Both Jesus and St. Paul consistently attended to the material care of those with whom they shared the Gospel, in the form of miracles and, in Paul's case, the collection for the poor in Jerusalem; we, as their successors, must do so as well. Nor does it suffice simply to assert that teaching of the faith must be accompanied by care for material well-being, as two distinct parts of the church's mission. There is an intrinsic relation between the two. The Gospel is the "good news to the poor" (Luke 4.18). With its message of hope and liberation, the Christian faith has concrete consequences in the life of the community.

These concrete implications are not strictly "economic development" in the way it is sometimes understood, with wealthier communities aiding those less fortunate (though they do not exclude this), any more than mission is necessarily a sending from more advanced societies to more marginal ones. They are, rather, a central aspect of the concrete discernment of the Gospel in communities of all kinds; spiritual transformation and material change go hand in hand. Allen recognizes this: "the activities of the Christians as individuals and as a body, the church in the place, should be the most clear revelation of the spirit... [W]hen [people] see a change in the lives of their neighbours...[t]hen the people are face to face with the Holy Ghost."[23] If Christians have at times neglected the integral nature of this connection, it is nonetheless true that it has had real manifestations throughout the world. Christian faith has been an integral (rather than incidental) force in efforts at

15

education, community development, advocacy, and revolution (two examples are considered below). Christian communities proclaim and participate in God's mission not simply or primarily in their words, but in their very lives.

The missiology that I propose, then, builds on Allen's insistence that the church follow the example of St. Paul in focusing on the communities in which mission takes place. It is a matter of nurturing and developing communities whose lives reveal God's reconciling purpose, albeit incompletely, to the world around them. To do this the church must address its Christian formation to the actual social and material situations of communities themselves and empower these communities to advance this formation themselves; that is, it must discern the truth of the Gospel in those specific contexts. Discernment does not relativize or undermine the Gospel. Rather, as Yoder argues, it is precisely the particularity of the Gospel, of Christ's lordship, that is professed in all new contexts, spoken in the language of pluralism. And in all contexts, appropriate humility and dependence on God's self-communication lead us to acknowledge that God is already present in all places and communities, waiting not to be revealed to them, but rather in them. This realization and the attendant goal of empowering communities themselves to witness to the Gospel in their own particular contexts together constitute the heart of Christian mission.

Mission so understood, as the proclamation of God's reconciling mission in the concrete lives of communities everywhere, does not take place exclusively, or even essentially, across national or cultural boundaries. Rather, it occurs wherever the life and ministry of the church constitutes a genuine testimony to the kind of reconciled, loving relationships that God desires for God's creatures. Nonetheless, encounters across various kinds of boundaries—which are often much closer than we imagine—can call us to understand just how radical and risky this reconciliation is, and are therefore a necessary component of our participation in mission. Further, they can remind us that the boundaries between the witnessing community and the world to whom it addresses its witness may be fluid and shifting.

Our participation in God's mission ultimately requires us to approach mission with an attitude of faith in the power of God in the Holy Spirit. It was this faith, according to Allen, that enabled St. Paul to entrust the formation and guidance of the early church to the communities themselves. Such trust is risky, and a more critical reading of Paul than Allen's suggests that the Apostle's example may be insufficient here. The trust and freedom that Allen finds so evident in Paul's dealings with the communities are firmly—and at times aggressively—circumscribed by Paul's insistence on the purity of the Gospel (this is perhaps most apparent in Galatians, the very text Allen cites as exemplary of Paul's emphasis on freedom!). Elsewhere, Allen attends to this concern for purity as he sees it in the missionary practices of his time.[24] He believes that such fear for proper doctrine expresses a lack of faith in the Holy Spirit, in the ability of others to receive the Gospel, and in the doctrine itself. The truths of Christian faith, he argues, are not primarily intellectual assertions, but are encountered in our experience. Thus the diverse experiences of faithful communities enrich, rather than threaten, doctrine.[25]

Allen urges us, therefore, to learn from the faith that grounded Paul's ministry. He argues that throughout his career Paul "believed in the Holy Ghost, not merely vaguely as a spiritual Power, but as a Person indwelling his converts. He believed therefore in his converts. He could trust them. He believed that Christ was able and willing to keep that which he had committed to Him."[26] While affirming the example of Paul's faith for contemporary mission, I would add the need to deepen it in the

17

way described above, balancing concern for purity with trust in the Spirit's ability to express the Gospel in new and diverse ways. God is active and revealing Godself in communities everywhere. The church is blessed with the opportunity to witness to and participate in this *missio Dei*, and to commend all of its efforts to God, trusting that God and God's people will together bring it closer and closer to fruition.

III. EXAMPLES OF MISSIONARY COMMUNITY

As a missionary of the Episcopal Church, I worked in Sitio de los Nejapa, a poor community in rural El Salvador. It is a place of great need, and its residents have been grateful recipients of a small number of charity and development programs. Yet when the few community leaders try to mobilize support for their own efforts, or to encourage new leaders, they are met with indifference. Many community members, particularly women with little formal education, attribute this apparent indifference to, among other things, feelings of inadequacy or lack of ability. They do not advocate on their own behalf, they say, because they are looked down on or ignored by local officials; they cannot be leaders because they lack the skills.

In weekly Bible studies, however, these women are able to encourage one another to value their own voices. In reflecting on passages such as Matthew 11.25 ("I thank you, Father…because you have hidden these things from the wise and the intelligent and have revealed them to infants") they begin to overcome their self-doubt and recognize their ability to speak for themselves. This new self-awareness, in turn, empowers them to collaborate with leaders of the church and community to develop other programs, such as a weekly sewing class.[27]

The story of the women of Sitio de Los Nejapa is an example of discernment of the truth of the Gospel in a specific context. The consequent changes, however slight, in the life of the community testify to more reconciled, equal relationships. Another, perhaps more striking, example can be seen in the well-documented, real impact of Christian base communities in Latin America. Don Pablito, a Salvadoran in the town of Cinquera, recounts how regular Bible studies initiated by local priests empowered community improvement: drunks stopped drinking, men stopped beating their wives, and workers began to advocate on behalf of their rights.[28] Again, discernment of the concrete implications of the Gospel creates a powerful witness to reconciled relations.

In both these examples, the material and social life of the community is one with its reflection on the truths of the Gospel, and constitutes its witness to the world. Here, in Allen's words, "the activities of the Christians as individuals and as a body, the church in the place, [are] the most clear revelation of the spirit." In some cases, this witness relies on the work of missionaries of some kind, persons whose work is to build up each community. Yet more fundamentally, the mission involved is the witness of the communities themselves, as their formation empowers them to proclaim to the world, through their shared life, the *missio Dei*.

IV. CONCLUSION

At its heart, Christian mission is participation in God's loving mission for all of creation. This participation is enacted in the lives of Christian communities everywhere, lives that bear witness to the divine purpose. In following Christ's example and testifying to ways of relating other than those that dominate society, believers are set apart from the world, as Christ was, in mission to it. This mission is integral to the identity of the church. The life of the church witnessing to the world: this is the foundation of mission, "the whole church bringing the whole Gospel to the whole world."

The character of that proclamation will be determined by the practices we use to shape our communities. Roland Allen's methods, focusing on the formation of viable communities, leadership from within, teaching that addresses particular, concrete contexts, and trust in the communities themselves and the Spirit working in them, offer some initial suggestions. Mission so understood provides a theologically compelling corrective to the impoverished conception that still leads some Christians, especially younger ones, to question the relevance of mission or reject it altogether. Christian mission is not intrinsically colonialist or hegemonic, but is rather the proclamation of God's presence in particular communities everywhere. This is good news in a world that sorely needs it.

END NOTES

1. Andrew R. H. Thompson is a Ph.D student in Religious Ethics at Yale University. With his wife, the Rev. Leigh Preston, he served as an Episcopal Missionary in El Salvador. He currently lives in West Hartford, and is active in the Episcopal Diocese of Connecticut.

2. These experiences are from my own time as a missionary in El Salvador with the Episcopal Young Adult Service Corps.

3. David Bosch, *Transforming Mission: Paradigm Shifts in Theology of Mission*, (Maryknoll, NY: Orbis books, 1991), 369-393.

4. Address by Rt. Rev. Stephen Bayne to Anglican Congress 1963, cited in Ian T. Douglas, "The Exigency of Times and Occasions," in *Beyond Colonial Anglicanism*, eds. Ian T. Douglas & Kwok Pui Lan (New York: Church Publishing, 2001), 28.

5. Bosch, 10.

6. Titus Presler, *Horizons of Mission* (Cambridge, MA: Cowley Press, 2001), 30; Bosch, *Transforming Mission*, 10, 370; Douglas, "Exigency," 42.

7. John Howard Yoder, *The Priestly Kingdom: Social Ethics as Gospel* (Notre Dame: University of Notre Dame Press, 1984).

8. Ibid, 92.

9. Ibid, 91, cf. Bosch 386.

10. John Howard Yoder, *The Politics of Jesus* (Grand Rapids, MI: Wm. B. Eerdmans, 1994), 94-97.

11. Yoder, *Priestly Kingdom*, 56.

12. Ibid, 49-54.

13. Ibid, 44.

14. Ibid, 59.

15. Roland Allen, *Missionary Methods: St. Paul's or Ours?* (Grand Rapids, MI: Wm. B. Eerdmans, 1962), 6.

16. Specifically, Allen discusses miracles (chapter 5), finance (chapter 6), preaching (chapter 7) and teaching (chapter 8). I have chosen to treat his accounts of Paul's teaching and use of finances together (based on a common emphasis on local autonomy) as "administration," and to change the order.

17. Allen, *Missionary Methods*, 83.

18. Ibid, 84-90.

19. Ibid, 91. Allen cites the ambiguous example of Paul's letter to the Galatians; problems with this reading will be noted below.

20. Ibid, 51-52.

21. Ibid, 62-64ff.

22. Ibid, 45.

23. Roland Allen, *The Ministry of the Spirit: Selected Writings of Roland Allen*, ed. David M. Patton (Grand Rapids, MI: Wm. B. Eerdmans, 1960), 100.

24. Roland Allen, *The Spontaneous Expansion of the Church and the Causes Which Hinder It* (London: World Dominion Press, 1927), 57-79.

25. Ibid, 66-67

26. Allen, *Missionary Methods*, 149.

27. The mission in Sitio de los Nejapa is still relatively young, too young to point to more dramatic outcomes. The sewing class has, at the time of this writing, come to an end, and the community members are working with the new missionary (a Salvadoran) to discern new possibilities for community engagement.

28 Interview with Don Pablito in Cinquera, El Salvador, November, 2007.

BIBLIOGRAPHY

Allen, Roland. *Ministry of the Spirit: Selected Writings of Roland Allen.* Edited by David M. Patton. Grand Rapids, MI: Wm. B. Eerdmans, 1960.

Allen, Roland. *Missionary Methods: St. Paul's or Ours?* Grand Rapids, MI: Wm. B. Eerdmans, 1962.

Allen, Roland. *The Spontaneous Expansion of the Church and the Causes Which Hinder It.* London: World Dominion Press, 1927.

Bosch, David. *Transforming Mission: Paradigm Shifts in Theology of Mission.* Maryknoll, NY: Orbis books, 1991.

Douglas, Ian T. "The Exigency of Times and Occasions." In *Beyond Colonial Anglicanism.* Edited by Ian T. Douglas & Kwok Pui Lan. New York: Church Publishing, 2001.

Presler, Titus. *Horizons of Mission.* Cambridge, MA: Cowley Press, 2001.

Yoder, John Howard. *Politics of Jesus.* Grand Rapids, MI: Wm. B. Eerdmans, 1994.

Yoder, John Howard. *Priestly Kingdom: Social Ethics as Gospel.* Notre Dame: University of Notre Dame Press, 1984.

2

Fallen is Babylon!
Missionary Conversion to God's Diversity

Christian Faith Among Other Faiths

Aaron Hollandar[1]

Our first task in approaching another people, another culture, another religion, is to take off our shoes, for the place we are approaching is holy. Else we may find ourselves treading on people's dreams. More seriously still, we may forget that God was there before we arrived.

~Kenneth Cragg

Any encounter with other religions needs to begin not with dialogue but with silence.

~Malachy Hanratty, SSC

M*etanoia*: repentance, conversion, reorientation. These are terms at the core of the Christian imagination. *Metanoia* implies the changing of *nous*, a Greek concept of the human interior—mind, heart, the perceiving self. A related term in the gospels is *epistrephein*, "to turn towards," which clarifies the meaning of conversion for the life of Christianity.[2] The

Church is called into being because of the need and capacity for conversion—turning—among the peoples of Creation: the requirement not of a 180-degree recoil from the movement of our lives, nor the abandonment of the communities that nurture us, but the reorientation of both towards new modes of being in relationship with each other and with God. In this vein, this essay is a study of conversion as a model for mission.

If the Church is called out to seek the *metanoia* of the world, then we must be careful not to understand this task as "conversion" in too narrow a sense. A venerable archetype of religious discourse is that of challenging the assumption that received religious belief and practice are being carried out appropriately.[3] In other words, the call for conversion has been and continues to be as meaningful within religious circles as it is between them. Missionary enthusiasm to convert others comes with the risk of forgetting the Christian commitment to *keep turning oneself* toward the new life—to convert the Church as part of the world. The Church in mission is participating in a process of the Spirit that calls it to share in the transformation it is working to inspire. Bishop Lesslie Newbigin is direct and insightful: "Jesus is not for one against the other. He is against all for the sake of all."[4]

1. Ears To Hear: The Significance of Inter-Religious Encounter

We can recognize in an earlier era of mission our truncated recognition of God in the unfamiliar; unfamiliar lands, peoples, and spiritual traditions represented a great challenge for the Church. When missionary churches' belief in the pre-eminence of their own heritage has been absolute, they have been in many cases unable to recognize the spiritual depth and relationship with God to which, for instance, tribal peoples patiently attested.[5] The possibility of discovering religious meaning on unfamiliar ground was precluded by a model of thinking that ranked what was already known above what was yet to be known.

However, careful attention devoted by the agents of mission to other religious milieus on their own terms reveals that human estrangement from the Divine, and the reconciliation and healing therewith, are indeed realities with more than one form. The (Christian, Aboriginal Australian) Rainbow Spirit Elders point out that "God does not speak to us first and foremost through European and Western theology"[6]—for instance, the brokenness of the land is the source of human alienation in this context, not the other way around (as in the prophetic tradition of Israel). A priori missionary suspicion of indigenous ways of knowing and relating to the sacred, supposing their insufficiency and need for Christian correction, was rooted largely in what we would identify today as confusion of a theological model with its subject of inquiry. The model in which the messages carried by natural phenomena, animals, and plants are read as seductive and false was certainly resonant for early Christian ascetics searching to be purified of earthly things in anticipation of the eschaton, but to call it a normative model is to call into question Christianity's applicability among cultures whose identity is closely and essentially bound to the land.

A few brief examples from the Missionary Society of St. Columban (SSC) will illustrate the dialogical processes and challenges at work in a more patient, open-ended approach to missionary interpretation of the other, both among indigenous peoples and other world religions.[7]

Many Columbans feel that, "to this day, most missionaries have not been adequately trained for dialogue;"[8] in other words, they tend at first to be bewildered by the realization that their "precious message" is but part of the total story of God's interaction with Creation. But despite any initial fears of relativism, the missionaries attest again and again that theological equilibrium is regained within this larger context. Witness to the gospel becomes part of the rhythm of relationship and discovery, rather than its prerequisite. For instance, the Columban missionaries in Lahore, Pakistan, worked through the mechanisms of the local government to launch an interfaith radio program in 2005. Waqt ki Awaz (The Voice of the Time) brings together interviews, radio dramas, discussions, and news; the radio format allows for interfaith concerns to be deposed from any academic or clerical pedestal and re-placed in "a dialogue of life" accessible to all.[9] Frank Hoare, a Columban in Fiji, became aware that Hindu Fijians were genuinely interested in Christians' experience of God. Seeking to meet this interest and bear his witness, he found that he could learn from a Hindu model of religious teaching: Fr. Hoare clothed himself in a sannyasi's (renunciate's) simple clothing and began to walk, sharing his vocation on no authority but that of his encounter with God. The missionary thus came to occupy a role in a non-Christian community that was not only permitted but encouraged.[10]

To some extent, argues John D'Arcy May, a fruitful encounter between Christianity and other spiritual systems "is only now beginning to take place."[11] That encounter begins with repentance and the demonstration that a change of life is taking place, combined with public and detailed commitment to the relationship. And to the extent that the encounter is more than a maneuver for power—if it is part of the Church's mission for the world, if it is carried out for the sake of God's Reign—it will allow the Church to be converted, deepened, oriented anew towards God's reconciling presence. Such *metanoia* is the possibility enshrined at the heart of Christianity; it is the great *charism* of the Church.[12]

2. THE HARVEST OF INSIGHT: MISSION'S MULTIDIRECTIONAL INCULTURATION

Religious creativity, both within a tradition and in that tradition's interactions with others, can be said to be more difficult, less secure, more disturbing and frightening, and ultimately far more rewarding than syncretism or eclecticism. It requires that traditions not merely be points of reference for contemporary life but that they *continue themselves to live*, and that those who adhere to them are faithful precisely by trusting their capacity to continue speaking—rather than repeating a recorded message. This speaking of ancient, culturally resonant symbols to new worlds of human understanding and interaction is at the foundation of Christianity itself: Jesus' calling forth of prophetic images and promises to be fonts of "living water," bearing the vision of messianic Sabbath and reconciliation into the contemporary terms of Roman occupation and Hellenistic Judaism.

In this light it needs to be noted that deliberate hybridity between religious imaginations, though often resisted as syncretism, cannot be unilaterally ruled out. The Rainbow Spirit Elders clarify this dangerous claim by pointing to the first chapter of John's gospel as an instance of just such hybridity: an inspired missionary document intended to convey the person of Christ in unprecedented metaphysical terms resonant to the particularities of Hellenic culture. John's gospel provides great insight into the early Church and its understanding of Christ's life; nevertheless, even with the gospel itself considered "catholic," universally valid, it must be recognized that identification of Christ with "Logos" is not. This identification, now beloved by Christians worldwide, began as a fortunate refraction through the prism of local experience. The Aboriginal translation of John 1:1-4 demonstrates the capacity of the gospel to live newly and speak in new ways when it is given its freedom to merge with different cultures and religious mentalities: "In the beginning was the Rainbow Spirit, deep in the land..."[13] Certainly the gospel according to John had this freedom, and we do not accuse it of syncretism.

Is there more to be learned of God? It seems the utmost arrogance to deny it. Bishop Newbigin is clear that when a pre-defined and immovable "verbal orthodoxy...becomes the supreme virtue [of religion], and syncretism becomes [its] most feared enemy,"[14] real dialogue and indeed, real mission are impossible. Much of the adultery language of the Hebrew scriptures was formulated out of the early Israelite conception of YHWH as a tribal god who would lift up his people against the rival gods of Canaan and Babylon; in this context, any kind of inter-religious collaboration can indeed be read as a betrayal. But today? Who is encountered by Christians among the chant and flames of a Hindu *puja*? If the ancient binary has merely shifted from "our God/their God" to "our God/*no* God," we have replaced tribalism with narcissism—no more. The risk of idolatry, reminds Gavin D'Costa, is much greater when "worshiping only the God of our own construction."[15]

The intercultural mission takes on a substantially expanded role when taking on this possibility (if not imperative) of genuine religious learning in the relationship with other faiths. As the wing of the Church that crosses over to dwell intentionally in extra-Christian communities, missionaries are on the front lines of inter-religious dialogue, going forth "both to teach and *be taught*,"[16] to serve the neighbor and to serve the Church by deepening its understanding of that neighbor, and indeed its own understanding of God. This task of mission has been articulated in different ways—or ignored, or anathemized—but that it has been a reality is beyond question. Sean McDonagh points out that the entire complex of liberation hermeneutics exists in modern Western churches because missionaries "brought back" liberation theology from Latin America.[17] This is only one example of what William Shenk calls the "harvest" of new insights from the mission-churches of this century, amounting to a "reformation" in their influence on the shape of the contemporary Church.[18]

So the corollary of co-creation between the missionary Church and the religious milieu in which it dwells is the mission's transmission of its new understanding, its own conversion, back into the flows of the global Church. This is not a marginal task: tireless work by theologians is needed for a kind of reverse inculturation, whereby the images and commitments of the churches are continually reinterpreted in light of the missions' deepening experience of the world—and deepening understanding of the truth enshrined but not owned by Christianity.[19] When new symbols are permitted to unfurl out of inter-cultural relationships and rally the maturing churches in new directions—only then can Christianity claim a commitment to catholicity.[20] Ecumenism, our relationality with the *whole* of the inhabited earth, asks us to communicate in new ways with ourselves as much as with our neighbors.

3. THE LOVING RISK: RELIGION AND RELATIONSHIP

"Now the whole earth had one language and the same words," begins the Genesis story of the Tower of Babel. Recalling the consequences of Babel's collapse, we might lament that not only the languages of communication but also the languages of human response to the Divine are confused and often mutually incomprehensible. However, this story speaks to us today as the hybrid of a cautionary tale and a prophetic affirmation: the construction of a world-kingdom out of a single stock—of language, vision, and cultural norms—is doomed by its very tendency to authoritarianism and uniformity. It is this temptation of Babel, which Newbigin calls the "archetype of all imperial adventures,"[21] that the story insists is abhorred by God, is torn down and replaced by total and frightening diversity with all its misperceptions, discomforts, and irreconcilable contradictions.[22]

I call this vision a prophetic affirmation from the perspective of Pentecost: Pentecost represents not the emergence and institution of a new universal language, a new foundation for the totalitarian union of humanity under a single banner, but rather the inspiration and flexibility by which the outpouring of the Spirit bears meaning in all languages. The miracle attested to is *the ability of the apostles to speak languages other than their own*; the passersby on the morning of Pentecost hear them speaking Parthian, Arabic, Phrygian, Egyptian, and in the idioms and nuances of these languages hear the deeds and message of Jesus affirming that the day of the Lord's favor is in their midst (Acts 2:1-11). Can we now trust that the oneness and right-ness of Creation envisioned as the Reign of God is characterized by its radical diversity, a Pentecost-character of all languages of meaning rather than a Babel-character of one supreme mode of understanding to which all others are subordinate? Can we conceive that the reality revealed in the gospel is broader than our grip on it, broader than the grip of the Church at large, is still being created through the interplay of Church and world, and will require not only the authority of the past but the dynamism of the present to be fulfilled?

When speaking of the relation of the Reign of God to religious experience beyond the Judeo-Christian imaginative field, we are not merely updating the "anonymous Christian" thesis. It is untenable to suggest that the world's religions are all oriented secretly towards the same soteriological vision proclaimed by the Hebrew prophets and lived by Jesus of Nazareth. The Kingdom is envisioned in the gospels as being *already* but also *not-yet*:

already, insofar as it is known and experienced in the life, death, and resurrection of Christ and the lives of his disciples, and not-yet, to the extent that it is *not* known, *not yet* experienced, *not* completely realized in the life of Christ, not predicted or understood by those who await its fullness. Even while, as Paul attests, those baptized in Christ are blessed with the "*arrabon*" (Eph 1:14) the "pledge" or "first-fruits" of the Reign, they do not know the shape of its universality. That which is universal, writes Martin Fuchs, must be "elaborated cooperatively" among all who are within its scope.[23]

Since Vatican II and the WCC assembly in Uppsala, we can affirm on broad ecumenical grounds that while Christians may conceive of salvation only through Christ, it is beyond our authority to rule out qualities of salvation *beyond* our conception. "The Kingdom of God," writes Jacques Dupuis, "is thus made up of all believers, Christian and otherwise, who in different ways, through various mediations, have heard the Word of God and received it in their hearts, and who have responded to the promptings of the Spirit and opened themselves to his life-giving influence."[24] Indeed this diversity is divine mandate: "Fallen, fallen is Babylon the great!" (Revelation 14:8).

This line of argument about God's Reign, though speculative and metaphorical, nonetheless renders an open-ended theology of religions legitimate. Because different faith-systems address themselves to *different questions* about identity, morality, relation to nature, and relation to God or Spirit or Source, the answers they provide should not be taken as contradictory *per se*; these questions may be framed in terms that make them appear the same, but given the cultural-linguistic context in which they are asked and the orienting narratives to which they contribute, they must be recognized as non-equivalent. "For the most intractable disagreements between the faiths of mankind are philosophical rather than religious. One culture has been built on a different view of existence from another."[25] A Buddhist asking, "Why is there suffering?" will provide a different answer to that of the Christian asking, "Why is there suffering?" but in addition is concerned with a distinct way of experiencing and processing "suffering"—is asking a different question. Thus the Christian answer does not "fulfill" the Buddhist question, although it may inspire a new direction of thinking and a deeper cross-cultural perspective. Another implication is that while the religions cannot be said to be strictly "contradictory," they also cannot be strictly "complementary," as if they were puzzle pieces that could be interchanged and fitted together as they are.

If the religions are neither contradictory nor complementary, what they are, then, is *relational*. Before we can expect any communication about religion with members of other faiths to bear significance, relationships must be established within which such conversation is appropriate. One of Christianity's most cherished affirmations is that the nations and cultures of the world are each other's kin, and deserve the unity and understanding that this familial context enables—and yet, such family relationships are complex, often painful, filled with paradox. The paradox of centuries of Christian mission was the deep sense of responsibility and familial love towards members of other faiths, expressed (recognizably, for anyone with siblings) through insistence on "I know best" and a paradigm of "you'll thank me later." We can ask, then: what are the qualities of mature relationship—relationship defined in the Christian worldview, moreover, by *love* even for those who do not seek to be loved and do not return love?

First, relationship requires a total commitment to listening, without presupposing an answer that suits us or justifies our current stance. Relationship requires, adds Paul Knitter, "that I have to confront [others] when I think they are wrong, but I also have to be authentically ready to be so confronted by them."[26] Being able to acknowledge that we do not always know best, even if we have never before been challenged in a particular way, is a pillar of any healthy relationship. Love "does not insist on its own way," writes St. Paul (I Corinthians 13:5). Love requires both commitment and discernment when going out from one's own space of comfort to encounter God in the foreign, the unknown.[27] It is a frustrating path, a frightening path, on which willingness to engage theologically with another's sacred texts and traditions "can never be a substitute for the more costly demands of friendship."[28]

Vinoth Ramachandra, writing these words in the context of Sri Lankan religious plurality and violence, has the experience of complex inter-religious relationship to support this claim. Friendship, solidarity, hospitality, shared living, shared bread, shared prayer: these are the ways of the Reign of God, and the necessary ground of any inter-religious dialogue lest that dialogue become so academic or sterile that its purpose is forgotten.[29] And to some extent, inter-religious relationship grounded in these qualities of life is itself a shared prayer, a reaching out to the Spirit welling up in the interstices of Creation's riot of interdependence—natural, cultural, and spiritual. In D'Costa's words, such prayer of life is "an act of loving risk, somewhat like Jacob's wrestling with the mysterious figure, whose identity is unknown and who refuses to be named."[30] To whom Jacob holds tight despite his strangeness, crying out "I will not let you go, unless you bless me" (Genesis 32:26). Who does bless the one who took the risk to have "striven with God and humans" (Genesis 32:28), yet never reveals his name. Whose name we may never come fully to know as we go on wrestling until dawn.

* * *

The mission of the Church is standing between two rooms, on the threshold, the door held open. As pilgrims, we continue on a rocky path, and as we "join with other believers in realising God's dream for our world"[31] by building communities of solidarity and shared life, we cannot but discover fresh meaning in our own deepest intentions and visions of wholeness. Yet there is a distinct core to the Christian revelation, and it is composed of more than its common ground with other revelations. The Christian story for the nations is a story in which the seemingly eternal powers of unjust dominion are not eternal, and in which the outcastes are brought home to table and restored to their dignity; it is a story of the earth whose immense history and groping complexity are not filled with vacant machines to be exploited but indeed are chosen as the dwelling place of the Divine.[32] When we speak of Christ as the presence of the Reign, we acknowledge that regardless of the Reign's interfaith and intercultural resonance it is fundamentally qualified by the Spirit that was unleashed upon the world in Judea.

In the prismatic light of Pentecost, shining on the toppled, hegemonic walls of Babel, the Church bears its witness to this story—but cannot do so by denying or belittling the presence of God in the rest of the world, nor by reaching theological conclusions on the "true nature" of "non-Christian religions" (as if those answers were readily available). The pilgrim Church need not repudiate others' articulations of truth in order to give witness to its own; the very meaning of "witness" is authentic testimony to experience and understanding, limited as it is, in the context of the witness of others. If the witness will not hear and consider the testimony of others, she ceases to be a witness and becomes a partisan ideologue.[33] Witness is not *authoritative*; if the Church desires authority over the other religions then it has strayed from following Jesus, who "emptied himself of status and took the form of a servant."[34] Evangelism, in the mindset I propose, is a function of kinship and service rather than assimilation.

The reconciliation at the heart of Christianity's vision is not just a restoration of a golden age or the re-enthronement of a long humbled people in exile; rather, "it brings us to a place where we have not been before."[35] This is the challenge of Edinburgh 2010: that of bearing witness to a Reign of God that exceeds our understanding, history, and experience—to which all peoples must be invited to participate in imagining. The story for the nations is still being written.

END NOTES

1. Aaron T. Hollander is a student of ecumenical theology and inter-religious relations from New York City, beginning the PhD program in Theology at the University of Chicago in September 2010. He currently serves as lay ecumenical officer and as a chorister for St. John's Episcopal Church, Brooklyn.

2. Paul Löffler notes that the relation between these two terms in the gospels and the book of Acts helps to clarify the process of conversion: for Luke especially, epistrephein marks the "moment" of turning, the rupture from a prior course, while metanoiein is the process of an individual's heart in flux. See Löffler, "The Biblical Concept of Conversion," p. 35.

3. This has been the case among today's constructive theologians, in the various historical reformations of the churches, in Jesus' challenges to the religious authorities,

and back to the poetic "guerilla warfare" of the Hebrew prophets (Brueggemann, *The Prophetic Imagination*, p. 75).

4. Newbigin, *The Open Secret*, p. 56. Elsewhere, Newbigin gives a definition of conversion that is consonant with work here: he writes that it is "a turning round in order to participate by faith in a new reality that is the true future of the whole creation. It is not in the first place either saving one's own soul or joining a society…If either of these things is put at the center, distortion follows" (cited without reference in Löffler, "The Biblical Conception of Conversion," p. 44). His point is that conversion is neither egocentric nor ecclesiocentric, but rather a process for the "whole creation"—both those who are being challenged and those who have historically done the challenging.

5. I use the example of indigenous religions here, although similar trends of misunderstanding marked early missionary encounters with Buddhists and Hindus as well, because of the devastating assumption among some missions to First Nations that certain (kinds of) cultures would have to be dismantled and reconstructed from the ground up in order to be saved. cf. Schreiter, *The New Catholicity*, p. 67.

6. The Rainbow Spirit Elders, *Rainbow Spirit Theology*, p. 6.

7. The SSC is an international, diocesan, Roman Catholic missionary society, which was established in 1919 to facilitate mission from Ireland to China. Today they are operational in many countries of Asia and Latin America, and live out a vibrant identity of open-hearted, inter-religious pilgrimage and solidarity with the poor—including the degraded and violated earth. In the summer of 2008, I spent time at the Columban

headquarters near Navan, Ireland, in order to study embodied missiology for my master's thesis in ecumenical studies.

8. Connolly, "An Evaluation of a Process of Strategic Planning in the Missionary Society of St. Columban," p. 3.

9. From a conversation with Fr. Colm Murphy in August 2008.

10 cf. Fischer, *Fiji Revisited*, p. 78-9. Fischer continues to describe the opening that was created by Fr. Hoare's willingness to step out not only from his homeland but from his inherited way of religious communication: "After listening to Father Hoare one day a Hindu said with enthusiasm: 'You're a guru, a teacher, a sannyasi! One of these holy men who comes out among us...'"

11. cf. May, *Transcendence and Violence*, p. 25. Many of the ecumenical landmarks of the last forty years have demonstrated the will to arrive at this point anew, even if hesitantly: the World Council of Churches' (WCC) assemblies at Vancouver (1983) and Canberra (1991), as well as its smaller convocations in Granvollen (1988) and Seoul (1990), sought to incorporate perspectives of First Nations people not as an exotic addendum to ecumenical work but as the realization of ecumenism's orientation in the manifold and interconnected earth.

12. As Vinoth Ramachandra succinctly puts it, "it is the gospel that enables [Christians] to humbly ask forgiveness from non-Christians for the sins of the Christian Church"—*The Recovery of Mission*, p. 273.

13. The Rainbow Spirit Elders, *Rainbow Spirit Theology*, p. 88. The whole passage is worth citing: In the beginning was the

Rainbow Spirit, deep in the land. And the Rainbow Spirit was with God, the Creator Spirit, and the Rainbow Spirit was God. The Rainbow Spirit was in the beginning with God. The Rainbow Spirit emerged from the land, transformed the land and brought all things into being on the land. With the Rainbow Spirit came life, and the life is the light of all people.

14. Newbigin, *The Open Secret*, p. 213.

15. D'Costa, *The Meeting of the Religions and the Trinity*, p. 144.

16. Knitter, *Jesus and the Other Names*, p. 145.

17. McDonagh, *The Greening of the Church*, p. 2. The Society of St. Columban observed even in 1982 that part of the missionary's work is "transmitting the vitality of the churches of the assignment" to the "home church" (The Columban General Assembly, *Columban Mission Today*, p. 39). This vitality, of course, involves the ever-developing influence of each local church's cultural heritage and religious milieu, and its unique insights into Christianity emerging from its life in community with particular others.

18. Shenk, "New Wineskins for New Wine," p. 73.

19. Schreiter notes that in many indigenous cultures that come to accept Christianity, the old ways are not supplanted but reinterpreted in light of the new revelation (*The New Catholicity*, p. 74). So too I am suggesting that for the churches to engage with their missionaries' experience of truth beyond their borders is not to abandon revelation in favor of pluralism or syncretism but to read each revelation to the world in the light of the insight of that world in its diversity.

20. David Bosch observes that until recently it was usually assumed that inculturation was a process only relevant to non-Western churches, that the gospel was perfectly "at home" in Europe and America (cf. *Transforming Mission*, p. 449). Now we can see differently, having been challenged to see that universality does not "belong" to anybody, and rather is open to all flows of the universe to which it claims relevance.

21. Newbigin, *The Open Secret*, p. 34.

22. The wordplay between my use of Babylon in the title of this essay and of Babel as a root-metaphor for its content is not arbitrary. Not only is Babel the name given to the historical city of Babylon in the Hebrew scriptures, but given the history of the Jewish people in captivity there, it is unthinkable that the tremendous Babylonian architecture would fail to impact their religious psychology. Observed through a history of religions lens, the mythos of Babel comes to evoke the arrogant political structure and towering ziggurats of Babylon. Likewise, the collapse of "Babylon" in the book of Revelation, a prophecy aimed squarely at the imperial hubris of Rome, employs resonances with the fall of Babel and the proleptic doom of all human authoritarianisms. Though this essay is too brief to include a full exegesis of and constructive response to Genesis 11, a particularly nuanced interpretation can be found in Miroslav Volf's *Exclusion and Embrace*, p. 226-231.

23. cf. May, *Transcendence and Violence*, p. 126.

24. Dupuis, *Christianity and the Religions*, p. 542. In this interpretation, therefore, inter-religious "dialogue takes place between people who already belong together in the Kingdom

of God" (ibid.). It is hardly radical to say that Christ is "wholly God, but not the whole of God" (Knitter, *No Other Name?*, p. 152); I am suggesting that it may also be said: he is "wholly Reign, but not the whole of the Reign."

25. Taylor, *The Go-Between God*, p. 184.

26. Knitter, *Jesus and the Other Names*, p. 39. An example that makes this point vividly clear is found in Vincent Donovan's account of preaching a sermon to the Masai people about overcoming tribal exclusivism and acknowledging God's love of reconciliation and the bridging of borders between people. At the end of the sermon, the cutting answer comes back: "Has your tribe found the High God?" In that moment, Donovan is in a state of true listening as well as proclaiming, in an authentic missionary state of relationship, and he himself experiences conversion, having been confronted with the tribal exclusivism of European Christianity. His response is sincere and represents the potential of Christians and non-Christians to move together in relationship to new understanding for each. He says: "No, we have not…But we are searching for him. I have come a long, long distance to invite you to search for him with us. Let us search for him together. Maybe, together, we will find him." See Donovan, *Christianity Rediscovered*, p. 45.

27. May's evocative term for inter-religious dialogue conceived on these terms is "the sacrament of the stranger"— *Transcendence and Violence*, p. 127.

28. Ramachandra, *The Recovery of Mission*, p. 272. These words, cited among a group of Columban missionaries (August 2008), brought instant recognition. Fr. Padraig

O'Donovan recalled a vivid recapitulation of the Good
Samaritan episode during his time in the Philippines: his
car having broken down at dusk many miles from home,
he watched as two busses drove by, driven by Christians
from his parish. The third bus driver was Muslim—who
stopped, and towed O'Donovan not only to a service
station but all the way home, past his own destination.
Fr. Sean McNulty told of his visit to a famous mosque in
Pakistan, whose imam had been disappointed at the lack
of visitors in the wake of political violence and reduced
tourism. Upon learning that this rare visitor was a Catholic
priest, the imam threw his arms around McNulty in a bear
hug, exclaiming "That's the best news I've had all month!"

29. Bühlmann argues that it is precisely this kind of academic
drift in inter-religious relations, promoting a common
ground that is little more than "classroom religion," that
makes such relations untrustworthy to so many (*The
Missions on Trial*, p. 34). D'Costa concurs, observing that
"there is something very disturbing about the reality of love
refusing to be controlled by our theorizing" (*The Meeting of
Religions and the Trinity*, p. 165).

30. D'Costa, *The Meeting of Religions and the Trinity*, p. 150.

31. The Columban General Assembly, *Columban Mission in the
Third Millennium*, p. 18.

32. cf. Revelation 21:3: "See, the home of God is among
mortals. He will dwell with them; they will be his peoples,
and God himself will be with them."

33. As Newbigin writes, "When the light shines freely one
cannot draw a line and say, 'Here light stops and darkness

begins.' But one can and must say, 'There is where the light shines...'" See *The Open Secret*, p. 198.

34. Stott, "The Biblical Basis of Evangelism," p. 7 (paraphrasing Philippians 2:7).

35. Schreiter, *Reconciliation*, p. 60.

BIBLIOGRAPHY

Aagaard, Johannes. "Mission after Uppsala 1968," in Anderson, Gerald H. and Stransky, Thomas F. (eds), *Mission Trends No. 1* (NYC: Paulist Press, 1974).

Bosch, David J. *Transforming Mission: Paradigm Shifts in Theology of Mission* (Maryknoll, NY: Orbis Books, 1991).

Boys, Mary C. "The Sisters of Sion: From a Conversionist Stance to a Dialogical Way of Life," in the *Journal of Ecumenical Studies* (Winter-Spring 1994).

Brueggemann, Walter. *The Prophetic Imagination* (Philadelphia, PA: Fortress Press, 1978).

Bühlmann, Walbert. *The Missions on Trial: Addis Ababa 1980* (Middlegreen, UK: St. Paul Publications, 1978).

The Columban General Assembly. *General Chapter 1970: Acts of the Chapter* (Dublin: Society of St. Columban, 1970).

------. *Columban Mission Today* (Dublin: Society of St. Columban, 1982).

------. *Becoming More Missionary: Our Shared Experience* (Dublin: Society of St. Columban, 1988)

------. *Columban Mission in the Third Millennium* (Dublin: Society of St. Columban, 2000).

------. *Strong and Courageous* (Dublin: Society of St. Columban, 2006).

Connolly, Noel. "An Evaluation of a Process of Strategic Planning in the Missionary Society of St. Columban" (Dublin City University: MBS Dissertation, 1993).

Cushner, Nicholas P. "Why Have You Come Here?": *The Jesuits and the First Evangelization of Native America* (Oxford University Press, 2006).

D'Costa, Gavin. *The Meeting of the Religions and the Trinity* (Maryknoll, NY: Orbis Books, 2000).

Donovan, Vincent J. *Christianity Rediscovered: An Epistle from the Masai* (London: SCM Press Ltd., 1978).

Dupuis, Jacques. "The Practice of Agape is the Reality of Salvation," in the *International Review of Mission* (October 1985).

------. "The Kingdom of God and World Religions," in Vidyajyoti (November 1987).

------. *Christianity and the Religions: From Confrontation to Dialogue,* trans. Phillip Berryman (Maryknoll, NY: Orbis Books, 2001 [orig.: Il cristianesimo e le religioni: Dallo scontro all'incontro (Brescia, Italy: Edizioni Queriniana, 2001)]).

Fischer, Edward. *Fiji Revisited: A Columban Father's Memories of Twenty-eight Years in the Islands* (NYC: The Crossroad Publishing Company, 1981).

Haught, John F. "Religious and Cosmic Homelessness: Some Environmental Implications," in Birch, Charles et al. (eds), *Liberating Life: Contemporary Approaches to Ecological Theology* (Maryknoll, NY: Orbis Books, 1990).

Knitter, Paul F. *No Other Name? A Critical Survey of Christian Attitudes Toward the World Religions* (London: SCM Press Ltd, 1985).

------. *Jesus and the Other Names: Christian Mission and Global Responsibility* (Maryknoll, NY: Orbis Books, 1996).

Koyama, Kosuke. "What Makes a Missionary? Toward Crucified Mind Not Crusading Mind," in Anderson, Gerald H. and Stransky, Thomas F. (eds), *Mission Trends* No. 1 (NYC: Paulist Press, 1974).

Löffler, Paul. "The Biblical Concept of Conversion," in Anderson, Gerald H. and Stransky, Thomas F. (eds), *Mission Trends* No. 2 (NYC: Paulist Press, 1975).

Lovett, Brendan. *A Dragon Not for the Killing* (Quezan City, Philippines: Claretian Publications, 1998).

Maxwell, Finbar. "The Experience of Transition and Human Personal Development in the Lives of Cross-Cultural Missionaries" (Loyola University Chicago: MA Dissertation, 2000).

May, John D'Arcy. *Transcendence and Violence: The Encounter of Buddhist, Christian and Primal Traditions* (NYC: Continuum International Publishing Group Inc., 2003).

McDonagh, Sean. *The Greening of the Church* (London: Geoffrey Chapman, 1990).

McFague, Sallie. *Metaphorical Theology* (Philadelphia, PA: Fortress Press, 1982).

McNulty, Sean. "Our Missionary Identity," in *Columban Intercom* 30.1 (2008).

Moltmann, Jürgen. *God in Creation* (London: SCM Press Ltd, 1985).

Newbigin, Lesslie. *The Open Secret* (Grand Rapids, MI: Wm. B. Eerdmans Publishing Co., 1978).

------. *Mission in Christ's Way: Bible Studies* (Geneva: WCC Publications, 1987).

Okure, Teresa. "'The Ministry of Reconciliation' (2 Corinthians 5:14-21): Paul's Key to the Problem of "the Other" in Corinth," in *Mission Studies* 23.1 (2006).

Panikkar, Raimundo. "The Christian Challenge to the Third Millenium," in Mojzes, Paul and Swidler, Leonard (eds), *Christian Mission and Interreligious Dialogue* (Lewiston, NY: The Edwin Mellen Press, 1990).

------. *The Intrareligious Dialogue* (Mahwah, NJ: Paulist Press, 1999).

The Rainbow Spirit Elders. *Rainbow Spirit Theology: Towards an Australian Aboriginal Theology* (Blackburn, Australia: Harper Collins, 1997).

Raiser, Konrad. *Ecumenism in Transition: A Paradigm Shift in the Ecumenical Movement*, tr. Tony Coates (Geneva: WCC Publications, 1991 [orig.: Ökumene im Übergang (Munich: Christian Kaiser Verlag, 1989)]).

Ramachandra, Vinoth. *The Recovery of Mission: Beyond the Pluralist Paradigm* (Carlisle, UK: Paternoster Press, 1996).

Schreiter, Robert J. *Constructing Local Theologies* (London: SCM Press Ltd., 1985).

------. *Reconciliation: Mission and Ministry in a Changing Social Order* (Maryknoll, NY: Orbis Books, 1992).

------. *The New Catholicity: Theology between the Global and the Local* (Maryknoll, NY: Orbis Books, 1997).

Shenk, William R. "New Wineskins for New Wine: Toward a Post-Christendom Ecclesiology," in the *International Bulletin of Missionary Research* 29.2 (2005).

Smith, Wilfred Cantwell. "Participation: The Changing Christian Role in Other Cultures," in Anderson, Gerald H. and Stransky, Thomas F. (eds), *Mission Trends* No. 2 (NYC: Paulist Press, 1975).

Taylor, John V. *The Go-Between God: The Holy Spirit and the Christian Mission* (London: SCM Press Ltd., 1972).

Tinker, George. "Spirituality, Native American Personhood, Sovereignty, and Solidarity," in the *Ecumenical Review* 44.3 (1992).

Volf, Miroslav. *Exclusion and Embrace: A Theological Exploration of Identity, Otherness, and Reconciliation* (Nashville, TN: Abingdon Press, 1996).

3

Returning Mission to Its Source: Our Duty in Palestine

Christian Communities in Contemporary Contexts

Annie Osborne[1]

I am writing on December 11, 2009. For most, here in the UK, it was a particularly ordinary December Friday. Usual British people were going about their usual life, preparing for Christmas, celebrating the end of university terms, or looking forward to a break from work. So it could have been for me, too, but my ordinary December Friday has been marked by two extraordinary events.

At lunchtime, I sang at a memorial service in thanksgiving for the life of an exceptional man, who spent his short life fighting against health troubles. Not only did he not complain, he also managed to touch the lives of many others through his altruistic commitment to his family, and to the wider society in his work as a lawyer. I never knew this man, and I know almost nothing of his personal faith, yet simply being present for his memorial was enough to make me realise that here was a truly godly man.

This evening, I was doing my end of term tidy-up, in the comfortable warmth of my shared student house and accompanied by my iTunes collection. Upon my Facebook news feed, there appeared a link to a website, which caught my attention. The website was http://www.kairospalestine.ps entitled "A moment of truth." This is a brand new statement written by a group of Christians in Palestine. The document is a plea to the world. Not just to the political world, but to the Christian world. It is a plea by a group of resistors, whose resistance continues without effect because it is not supported.

This essay will take these two apparently unconnected events to explore of what Christian mission is, and why it may be as important today for us to tend to older ground as new.

"BUT FIRST OF ALL, PLEASE, LET THERE BE LOVE"[2]

I shall begin by outlining the life of an exceptional man. To us, he may remain anonymous, because each and every human, created in the image of God, is given the opportunity to emulate such a man. This man was born with glaucoma, affecting his eyesight so badly that doctors worried he would never see. With the support and expertise of a doctor in his hometown, he was given partial sight. This enabled him to go on to great achievements, and he stepped out of university into a law job in the city, without a trace of pride. This was his way of serving the world, of repaying the debt of gratitude he had for having survived, and seen.

He went on to enjoy the natural world, first in the mountains and later developing a partiality for sailing, together with his brothers and friends. He married, and had one daughter. Both wife and daughter loved horse riding, about which he knew very little. Yet his joy was no less, whenever they achieved success in a race. His career as a busy London solicitor and his interest in radio led him to be at the heart of the success of one of the greatest radio businesses in the UK. We heard moving tributes to him, today, from top lawyers and media directors who valued him both as a colleague and as a friend. His daughter, seventeen years old, today gave thanks for "the best father you could ever wish to have."

Through all of this, our extraordinary man was suffering from an extraordinary health condition, which was beyond even the most expert doctors in this country's hospitals. He bore it with patient acceptance. He never gave up his job, he never gave up his sense of humour, sending a text message to his brother while in an ambulance on his last day, declaring that the journey was "v. exciting."

The story may begin to sound sentimental; but there is a lesson that we may all learn from such a life. Our extraordinary man achieved his extraordinary life because he possessed four things: belief, love, support, and determination. Belief in his ability to make the world a better place; love for (and from) his family, his friends, his job; support from all with whom he came into contact, above all his wife and his doctors; determination to continue making the most out of life, even when life put obstacles in his way. These were his gifts, from God, which he put to the service of those around him.

And are these not also the ingredients of mission? A belief, above all in God's goodness, and in our ability to bring the gift of Christ into the life of our fellow humans; a love for all, regardless of their creed, culture, colour or condition; a support from our friends and neighbours and for the hardships that many must suffer, through poverty, violence, discrimination; support from the same God who says "behold, I am with you always, to the end of the age;"[3] and a determination to spread God's glory through the world—to "make disciples of all the nations"[4]—despite the challenges it may present.

He was no missionary in an official sense, but this man spent his life demonstrating the gifts of God to the world, and there can be no doubt that this mission touched all those who came into contact with him. And it is that mission, those gifts, which are the very ingredients necessary for the successful, holy peace that is sought by the writers of today's Kairos document.

"TELL ME THAT YOU'LL OPEN YOUR EYES"[5]

"Jerusalem, city of reconciliation, has become a city of discrimination and exclusion" (1.1.8).[6] Now, Jerusalem and the Holy Land have never been places of peace and tranquillity; for centuries upon centuries they have survived conflict: "Jerusalem a desolation".[7] Much of that conflict has been, and continues to be, a matter of religious hatred: "Israeli settlements ravage our land in the name of God" (1). Still this continues, and somehow although we condemn it *officially*, those of us who live in Europe and the West seem to take this conflict for granted. We acknowledge that it is atrocious, but treat it as 'their problem' or 'insoluble' and continue about our 'good Christian lives'.

But the conflicts in the Middle East are a source of "daily humiliation" which make "family life impossible" in a place where even "freedom of access to the holy places is denied" (1). Respect, family, prayer: three aspects of a dignified human life. Three aspects of life that are consciously promoted and nurtured by our missionaries, who go out to new communities and teach their members about these values through the word of God.

"We see nothing in the present or future except ruin and destruction," write these Palestinians in paragraph 3.2, "we see the upper hand of the strong, the growing orientation towards racist separation and the imposition of laws that deny our existence and our dignity." It is a bleak outlook indeed, and one that is fuelled by fundamentalist misuse of the very faith that we share and that we have a mission to promote: "…the word of God is petrified and transmitted from generation to generation as a dead letter. This dead letter is used as a weapon in our present history in order to deprive us of our rights in our own land" (2.2.2).

It is unsurprising that those who are able to leave do so. And so "the land is deprived of its most important and richest resource—educated youth" (1.3). And what sort of hope may remain in a country whose youngest, most energetic, most capable individuals have themselves lost their determination and felt lacking in the necessary support to defend their dignity?

The document we read today is a desperate plea, from a deeply faithful, loving community. Their faith is steadfast: "we believe that the Word of God is a living Word, casting a particular light on each period of history, manifesting to Christian believers what God is saying to us here and now" (2.2.2). "…We renew our faith in God because we know that the word of God can not be the source of our destruction" (2.3.4).

These people are not fighting against any religion, nor are they making an enemy of their fellow countrymen: "our message to the Muslims is a message of love and of living together and a call to reject fanaticism and extremism. It is also a message to the world that Muslims are neither to be stereotyped as the enemy nor caricatured as terrorists but rather to be lived with in peace and engaged with in dialogue" (5.4.1). There is no question of needing to form a solely Christian community: "Our presence in this land, as Christian and Muslim Palestinians, is not accidental but rather deeply rooted in the history and geography of this land […] It is God's land and therefore it must be a land of reconciliation, peace and love. This is indeed possible. God has put us here as two peoples, and God gives us the capacity, if we have the will, to live together and establish in it justice and peace" (2.3.1, 2.3.2) These people are struggling with a generalised lack of love and respect in their country, not with any religious practise or belief.

And despite all that they are going through, these people still have hope: "Today, we bear the strength of love rather than that of revenge, a culture of life rather than a culture of death. This is a source of hope for us, for the Church and for the world" (3.4.5). A hope that is derived from a faith, and that gives them the determination to carry on, to toil endlessly to reach "a new world in which there is no fear, no threat, but rather security, justice and peace" (1.4). "We believe that God's goodness will finally triumph over the evil of hate and of death that still persist in our land. We will see here "a new land" and "a new human being", capable of rising up in the spirit to love each one of his or her brothers and sisters" (10). Their appeal is for the very essentials of a loving, peaceful world. They do not ask for anything beyond our call as Christians working for the good of God's people. Is it something we expect to be asked for? And did we need to wait to be asked?

"Money can't buy me love"[8]

What are we, European Christians, of all denominations, currently *doing*, for these people who share our beliefs and strive for the good of their community but whose lives are deprived of such essential elements as love and respect? Could it be that we are investing our money, but not our love, in the Holy Land? Have we given up hope for the end of a conflict, while those who have to endure it from day to day remain loving and faithful and above all, hopeful? Whatever our attitude, it is shameful indeed to ignore a need for love and support, as shameful as if we were to allow our dear lawyer friend to live through his illness unsupported and unloved. Our mission as Christians is not only to bring God's word and God's love to the "heathen." It is to surround the whole of God's people with his love, and to use it as a tool for peace.

These people are appealing because they lack support from outside, they lack attention from the Church, they are powerless without the greater Christian mission of *love* supporting and believing in their goal. Love is their word, love is their request, love is their prayer. "Our numbers are few but our message is great and important. Our land is in urgent need of love" (5.4). These Palestinians firmly believe that if they are shown this love, if enough work can be done through love in their land, then their land will finally be a place where Christian, Muslim, Jew, any human can live a dignified life, peacefully, alongside his neighbours, without fear or humiliation.

> Resistance is a right and a duty for the Christian. But it is resistance with love as its logic. It is thus a creative resistance for it must find human ways that engage the humanity of the enemy…and thus achieve the desired goal, which is getting back the land, freedom, dignity and independence … with methods that enter into the logic of love and draw on all energies to make peace. (4.2.3, 4.2.5, my emphasis)

It is not the first time that such statements have been issued. They do not make exhilarating reading. But this is not an academic essay, to be swept aside among papers on a dusty desk. It is a call to us all to open our ears and eyes, to recognise that peacekeeping is not only about money, about political speeches, or about military intervention. It is also about love.

"Here I am, send me"[9]

Numerous prophets and apostles have been missionaries: one was St. Paul, who went on a mission to bring the people of the

Mediterranean into the Christian fold. We, usual British people, have St. Paul to thank—in part at least—for the way we live our lives today, which regardless of our personal beliefs, have been shaped by centuries of Christian thought in Western Europe.

Since Paul's time, generations upon generations of Christians have followed missionary vocations to locations more or less exotic, more or less accepting of foreigners, more or less open to receiving the word of God. Those people have put their belief, their love, their support and their determination into nurturing new communities of faith. They have also relied on a strong support from their own home communities, without whom they would have neither the resources nor the determination to continue their work.

St. Paul's mission began in the Middle East, and the Middle East was indeed the birthplace of mission: "God sent the patriarchs, the prophets and the apostles to this land so that they might carry forth a universal mission to the world" (2.3.1). Today, the people of the Middle East are crying out, and their cry is essentially for that mission to return to its source. Let us hear it.

> The mission of the Church is prophetic, to speak the Word of God courageously, honestly and lovingly in the local context and in the midst of daily events. If she does take sides, it is with the oppressed, to stand alongside them, just as Christ our Lord stood by the side of each poor person and each sinner, calling them to repentance, life, and the restoration of the dignity bestowed on them by God and that no one has the right to strip away. (3.4.1)

Part of our service as Christians is to fulfill that mission that God sends us each on, to spread the good news of his love to every corner of the earth. As members of the body of Christ, we "cannot favour or support any unjust political regime, but must rather promote justice, truth and human dignity" (3.4.3).

As such, we are called to attend to the Palestinian situation. We must respond to their cry.

> Our question to our brothers and sisters in the Churches today is: Are you able to help us get our freedom back, for this is the only way you can help the two peoples attain justice, peace, security and love? (6.1)

Surely we are able. We should not be frightened of the dangers associated with assisting a people in a situation of violence and oppression, favouring an idyllic 'missionary' placement in a far away country where we can send photos of our little children back to our home church, to be marveled at because of the exotic setting, with letters about how our Bible translation into a language we hardly know is doing.

In their message, they invite us to "come and see" (6.2). Just as St. Paul took care to return to troubled areas rather than always moving forward to new communities, so we must turn around. It is time for a rebirth of Christian mission, turning away from goody-goody tourism and returning to the source, to address our mission, as Christians, to offer love and support where it is most needed. To live as examples of God's love, in the hopes that those examples will 'convert' wherever is required. Those conversions may not be overt conversions to the Christian faith: we may not be able to send home proud statistics related to numbers of baptisms, or take photographs of a lively congregation on Sunday morning. Our mission of love may recruit only to the invisible church. But with the Church Fathers, I believe that the invisible church is also God's church, and if we can change the world for our fellow Christians, and for their neighbours of all faiths, by sewing seeds of love where there was hostility and violence, then this is our mission.

If we stand by, if we engage in mission only elsewhere in the world, in places where God seems unknown, but where people live their daily life with no immediate threat to their dignity, we are offending against the very meaning of our Christian mission. We are lacking the love of God. We are working selfishly for a visible gain, for countable conversions. We are not listening to the needs of our world.

Let us now return mission to its source and, like the man whose life, so ordinary, was one of love, faith, support and determination, live as true Christians regardless of our title. Let us go out into the world and show all people the love of our Lord who himself was willing to endure death on the cross for the good of the world. Let us rebuild Jerusalem.

END NOTES

1. Annie Osborne is from Cambridge, U.K. She received her first degree from Cambridge University, and is about to complete her MA in Literary Translation at the University of East Anglia (UEA) in Norwich, translating literary prose and poetry from French and Italian.

2. "Let there be love"—Lionel Rand & Ian Grant (1940).

3. Matthew 28: 20 tr. English Standard Version, Anglicised Edition (2002)

4. Matthew 28: 19 tr. English Standard Version, Anglicised Edition (2002)

5. "Open your Eyes"—Snow Patrol, Eyes Open (2006)

6. Numbers refer to paragraphs in the document *A Moment of Truth* (December 11, 2009) published at www.kairospalestine.ps

7. Isaiah 64:10 tr. English Standard Version, Anglicised Edition (2002)

8. "Can't buy me love" — Lennon/McCartney (1964)

9. "Here I am send me"—Delirious? Now Is the Time (2006)

4

The Primacy of the Message of Love in a Postmodern World

Mission and Postmodernities

Ariel Siagan[1]

The era of postmodernism opens a door of opportunities for the Church to emphasize love as its primary message. It is a kind of love that motivated God to save the world.[2] It is the same love that the postmodern generation needs to know. Postmodernism is defined by Merriam-Webster dictionary as the era after the modern one.[3] It was during the modern period that the western world has structured society based on universal and absolute values, applying scientific and rational processes. On that background, postmodernism discredited the absolution of values and questioned science and rationale processes. One of the loud voices heard was that of Jean-Francois Lyotard when he defines postmodernism:

> ...as incredulity toward metanarratives. This incredulity is undoubtedly a product of progress in the sciences: but that progress in turn presupposes it. To the obsolescence of the metanarrative apparatus of legitimation corresponds, most notably, the crisis of metaphysical philosophy and of

the university institution which in the past relied on it. The narrative function is losing its functors, its great hero, its great dangers, its great voyages, its great goal.[4]

Postmodernists encourages an attitude of distrust toward institutional structures and promotes suspicion toward the universal and absolute values set by the modern times; even the Biblical narratives were put into criticism. As a result a person in the postmodern era becomes alienated to the structures of society, losing the individual's sense of meaning in the process. The Bible is prophetic when the teacher laments of the meaninglessness of life, after he has seen and achieved everything. He said everything is utterly meaningless.[5]

But it is just one side of the two-facet coin. The fact that third world countries never experienced modernization, the word 'postmodernism' takes on a whole new and different meaning. Ambivalence would be felt at the mention of it, since the very context of its definition can be found in European and North American experience, but never here. Looking at this location, post modernism started when globalization was introduced as the new world economic rules of engagement. It is viewed as part of a continued trend of occupying and dominating the land and its people by the powerful countries with a purpose of expansion to established new markets and sourced out raw materials. The Church being a part of the society has been instrumental in achieving its goal. The message the Church's emphasis varies from time to time depending on the prevailing economical and political paradigm.

Being a young Christian living at the context of postmodernism in the third world setting, I found myself doubting the meta-narratives that shaped the values and beliefs I learned from the Church. Instinctively I undergo a process of deconstruction, putting into close scrutiny the reasons behind reason to find meaning for my existence. Looking at the biblical narratives that gave sense to my being as against the messages of realities that surround me, I found everything in conflict.

It is imperative that the Church offers a refreshing message to the postmodern generation to address the alienation of the individual in the affluent societies, and the suffering of the poor and oppressed in different societies. We can offer the message of love, manifested in the truth of our interconnectedness, as against the message of individualism, which alienates the person to the world and its realities. Similarly, we can offer the message of love discernible in Christ pursuit of reconciliation as an opposition against the message of expansion that seeks to dominate the other.

This paper is a product of careful introspection and critical inspection of the location I am living now. With intentional bias, I will narrate manifestations of postmodernism in the third world setting. The dynamics of globalization will be scrutinized, as it is one of the forms of postmodernism phenomenon. Why do we need to emphasize the message of love? And, what are its contents? Together let us try to look for answers.

BIBLICAL NARRATIVES VS POSTMODERN NARRATIVES

The church has embedded a sense of direction and purpose in my life. Our Sunday school provided me biblical stories that shaped the very core of my being. One of the great stories I learned is the story of God who so loved the world that He gave his only begotten son, so that if I believed I will not perish but have an everlasting life[6] and life in its fullness.[7] To restore and redeem what has been destroyed and stolen, he became incarnated as a human, became just like us, died on the cross and rose again, saving us from the inevitability of sin and death. It is love which motivated God to reach us. These narratives have programmed my life, and its rationale guided my decisions.

Contrastingly, the sweet narratives of the Bible are set in a bitter situation of today's world economic and political systems. The present realities are coherently stating a narrative of domination of the economically powerful nations to the economically weak countries. Notably, there is a direct connection to colonization and globalization, and the messages propagated by the Church in a certain locus. Historically, the western countries pioneered the missionary trail in the modern times. A Christian conference in Edinburgh in 1910 had been the starting point of systematic method of missions to the countries that doesn't have a Christian formation. The missionary zeal of our forebears gave birth to the creation of today's church structure in Africa, North and South America, Europe, Asia and the Pacific; my home included. It can never be denied that the same structures, and the message they carried, increased the vulnerability of the indigenous people to succumb to foreign domination. Eventually colonies received their independence only to be subjugated by the then 'new world order' called globalization.

A description from a third world perspective states clearly: "globalization puts the centricity of people under the centricity of free or untrammeled markets. It allows the lumping together of non-homogenous economy into a single global market."[8] Thus, resulting in the suffering of many who cannot compete in a global market. Globalization attached messages of hope and prosperity to its transnational corporations that give jobs to many in third world countries. With the aggressive expansion of businesses through the ethos of globalization came a new church movement that has the same aggressiveness for expansion through missions. Charismatic movements flourished at the location where structures of globalization are present. Notably the messages they deliver puts emphasis on individualism and the individual's capacity to rise the ladder of success in a corporate setting. I observed that in the Philippines, their messages are appealing to the young people who desire to have a great career. It also appeals to the tiny middle and upper classes that are economically stable. On the other hand, the economically challenged segment joined in to churches that preached prosperity gospel. The movement was so strong that it changed the perception of the people towards Church. It also challenged the landscape of inter-church engagements as well as the missionary understanding of the people inside it. Churches nowadays exist like a business entity. I remember visiting one of the big cities in Southeast Asia. As I curiously look from my vehicle I saw numerous church billboards, along business establishments. Those billboards seemed to be competing with each other as against to the churches in the whole stretch of the highway, all proclaiming their own brand of Christianity. One banner speaks of Jesus as 'the healer', an enticement to those who seeks emotional, spiritual as well as physical healing, while another delights for preaching a Bible-based teachings and Christ-centered theology. The impression it left with me, or for anyone who will be passing that highway, was that the individual is a consumer, while the church is the business enterprise and God is a piece of merchandise. What kind of messages does the world hear from us as a Church? Is the Church being shaped by the paradigms of the location within which it belongs?

This testifies to what Zygmunt Bauman described, that ours is a consumer society where members of the society are being judged by their ability and willingness to play that role.[9] The messages being heard from our churches is complimenting the current trend of globalization and supporting the intensification of consumerism. Consumerism reduces a human person to a mere consumer. The present milieu puts importance and value of 'having over being'. Young people are driven to advance their careers. The measure of success is centered on the achievements and how much a person is earning monetarily. But it seems a dead-end road. The human quest for meaning is found to be futile in a postmodern world. This generation put irreconcilable suspicion to the structures and institutions that once gave them meaning. Instead young people are turning to new age movements that would cater to their personal lifestyle and preferences to provide them meaning. Rev. Dr Peter Churchley-Jones described a Western experience as a woman spoke to her, "It used to be that everyone went to Church, now you are the odd one out if you go."[10] People nowadays are looking at the structured church with doubt. The exponential growths of alternative religions are clear signs of this pluralistic society. Are our churches failed to bear witness of Christ's love to this generation, or are our messages pulling people away? The history of division and schisms in our churches puts a negative impact on how this generation, particularly the Western societies, perceive the church.

There has never been, in the history of human society, such a heavy atmosphere of distrust which affecting human interactions. Young people are especially vulnerable to alienation. Commercial establishments called it individualism to sugarcoat the idea. The meteoric rise of people consulting psychological clinics and the heavy usage of real time strategy games are clear signs of an alienated generation. The frequent visits of people to online social networking sites could also be credited to that. I am not an exception on this trend. Social networking sites provide us a venue to escape realities and create a paradigm of our own, which is different and potentially much better than the world around us. Does consumerism causes this dreadful phenomenon? How are we going to use the Internet as a platform to reach out to this generation? What emphasis on our messages should they hear?

Looking deeply at the issue of consumerism, we can locate another reigning issue of our time, the issue of climate change, which can be traced to the degradation of our environment due to the extraction of natural resources. We have never seen magnanimous typhoons and hurricanes that are happening now. I experienced it first-hand. Nothing in my memory could be compared to the fury of Typhoon Ketsana that hit Metro Manila and its surrounding provinces one fateful evening in October 2009. Poor people living near low-lying areas were swept by the astonishing amount of rainfall that it submerged majority of the region by a 20 feet flood. On one of our church disaster relief operations, I remember a father who lost his wife and 2 sons. His anguish is obvious but understandable. What is not understandable is the fact that thousands of lives were lost and millions around the globe are suffering because the earth we inhabit has been destroyed by our overt consumerism. Third world countries are not capacitated to mitigate the effects of climate change. Different church and church agencies are responding through relief operations, projecting a message that 'we care'. Although it will just be temporary solutions to a deep-seated problem originating from globalization and the consumerist culture it promotes.

The Church's response should go beyond providing temporary solutions. Our messages should address not only the victims of climate change, but also the proprietors of globalization in order to be credible. Though violent resistance is oftentimes applied on it. Even the church was not spared from harassment and violence. I remember an encounter with a community where a priest was abducted and tortured before being killed because he devotedly mobilized his parish, who are mostly indigenous people, against the construction of foreign-invested mining site. Torn by the death of their loving priest, the community held several prayer vigils denouncing their own government's inability to dispense justice, as well as their direct participation in the killing. This violence, characterized by heavy militarization, can also be found happening in the countries of Rwanda and in the Democratic Republic of Congo and in Iraq.

Despite all its tangible negative effect on ecosystem and the human person, globalization remains unaddressed. Unable to rise from the prevailing economic order, people from Third World countries seek employment in the first world countries in exchange of relatively high salary. People from the South and Southeast Asia became domestic workers in Hong Kong and in the Middle East. I have seen nurses, even top-notch medical doctors, who are heading to the United States and United Kingdom pursuing 'greener pasture', while abandoning their nationalistic duties. This has caused 'brain-drain' to the already mineral-drained country. What is ironic is that the educational system of the Philippines produced a large number of competent health care providers, while majority of the people do not have access to health care. Forced migration because of poverty has been accounted for keeping the Philippine economy afloat, despite worldwide economic recessions. This phenomenon negatively disintegrates the family and degraded a human person. How then can we address the structure of power that seeks to dominate the poor? What messages could we offer to this broken postmodern world?

CONCLUSION

The emphasis on the message of love seems too weak to counter the prevailing messages of aggressive expansion testified by the current trend of globalization. But studying communication processes, the strength of the message largely depends on the credibility of the one sending it. Are the churches today not credible enough to address the current system of expansion that oftentimes involves coercion? On a careful analysis, we can say that the Church has been supporting this system of living. We can trace it from colonization period up to this moment of time. Has the church been too weak to denounce it? The emphasis on the message of love becomes now more compelling and appropriate, as it demands discernment and action in order to dispense justice and promote equity of resources. It is not just showing that we care, but more importantly it is saying that our lives are interconnected; therefore whatever I have is yours and whatever is yours are mine. Interconnectedness is not limited among humans, but has its application to all the created order. The message of love is the message of sharing. It defies human tendency to be greedy, and promotes co-existence among all creatures. The message of love will not be completed without the dispensation of justice. The Church has to be hands-on in the promotion, and in its advocacy for a just and humane society. Corrupt economic structures must be exposed and confronted. Imperatively, we need to provide alternative ways of living based on our interconnectedness. The Bible has a point to offer, it was the story of a boy who is willing to share his five loaves of bread and two fishes with everyone. Jesus prayed for it and has it distributed to almost five thousand men, beside women and children. When everybody is full, astoundingly, they had collected 12 basketfuls of leftovers.[11] Multiplication of our resources happened when we are willing to share.

The message of love is also a message of reconciliation.[12] An emphasis on the message of love, expressed in God's ministry of reconciliation against the current trend of individualism, addresses the sense of alienation and meaninglessness of today's generation by pondering on the reality that an individual is part of a community. God designs a human person to function in communion with others. God reconciles us to Himself and then to others. The ministry of reconciliation ascertains a degree of acceptance, as well as tolerance, to different practices of life-affirming religions and beliefs, in acknowledgement that God works in the hearts of individual, the community, and the nation in ways we may not recognize. This message also suggests that we reflect on church unity as an expression of love towards all; the interconnected order.

"And now these three remain: faith, hope and love. But the greatest of these is love."[13] The postmodern era provides the Church opportunity to re-define its message of love and to put emphasis on it to reach out to this generation. We may have been alienated by the word 'love', but putting it into the context of the Bible and the traditions of the Church; the word 'love' has a significant meaning to the overall mission of God. It is time to redeem and examine the beauty of its meaning, and it is time to align the missions program of our church based on the message of love. Perhaps it is the only message that every generation, including the past, needs to know.

END NOTES

1. Ariel G. Siagan is a member of the Iglesia Evangelica Metodista En las Islas Filipinas (IEMELIF). He is currently a volunteer of the Christian Unity and Ecumenical Relations Unit of the National Council of Churches in the Philippines.

2. The nature and mission of the Church, World Council of Churches, Geneva.

3. Merriam Webster Online Dictionary.

4. Jean-Francois Lyotard, The Postmodern Condition: A report on Knowledge, 1979.

5. Ecclesiastes 1:2. NIV.

6. John 3:16, NIV.

7. John 10:10, NIV.

8. The National Council of Churches in the Philippines, Towards A Common Vision and Mission, Quezon City, March 1998.

9. Zygmunt Bauman, 'The Self in a Consumer Society' published by *The Hedgehog Review*, 1999.

10. Rev. Dr Peter Churchley-Jones, *With a Demonstration of the Spirit and of Power*, WCC Publications, Geneva, Switzerland, 2004.

11. Matthew 19:14-21. NIV.

12. 2 Corinthians 5:18, NIV.

13. 1 Corinthians 13:13, NIV.

5

Jesus' Third Way as the Central Model for Building Peaceful Community in Myanmar

Mission and Power

Hau Sian Suan[1]

The long history of Myanmar is full of sorrow, with people who are frightened, oppressed and exploited. All the people in Myanmar are in deep sufferings, not only by the evil system of the Government, but also by catastrophes like the *tsunami* and Nagris. Within this painful situation, the Christian proclamation of the Good News is the inevitable task of not only the ministers, but every Christian as well. Christians are being even more challenged by the religious-pluralistic society that exists within Myanmar. In this chaotic situation, there arise many questions like: *What is the essence of Christianity, and how can people find their dignity in an unjust society?* However, in the Bible, Jesus Christ has shown the Way—to overcome sufferings, to be a dynamic Christian present in the society, and to build a peaceful Community in Myanmar—is to love and to resist the enemy nonviolently.

1. RELATED NEW TESTAMENT CONCEPT

Luke depicts the disciples requesting permission to call down fire from heaven on inhospitable Samaritans; Jesus rebukes them (Luke 9: 51-56). When Peter cuts off the ear of the high priest's slave in an attempt to save Jesus from arrest, Jesus is shown commanding, "No more of this!" (Luke 22:51)—an injunction the church took literally for the next three centuries. Matthew has Jesus saying, "Put your sword back into its place; for all who take the sword will perish by the sword" (Matt. 26:52). Turning the other cheek to a "superior" who has backhanded an "inferior" is an act of defiance, not submission; stripping naked when a creditor demands one's outer garment brings down shame on the head of the creditor for causing the poor debtor's nakedness; carrying a soldier's pack a second mile would put him in violation of military law (Matt. 5:39-41). These acts do not at all mean acquiescing passively in evil, but are a studied and deliberate way of seizing the initiative and overthrowing evil by the force of its own momentum.[2]

The Last Supper and the Crucifixion display Jesus' nonviolent breaking of the spiral of violence by absorbing its momentum with his own body. What Jesus distilled from the long experience of his people in violent and nonviolent resistance, was a way of opposing evil without becoming evil in the process. He advocated means consistent with the desired end: a society of justice, peace and equality free of authoritarianism, oppression, and ranking. His method and his goal incarnated God's domination-free order.[3]

Jesus proclamation of God's domination-free order provides a framework for dealing with the role of the churches in helping nations move from autocracy to democracy. Far more is at stake than merely an orderly transition to a more representative form of governance; such in history open up to heavenly potentials.

They are transparent to the possibility of the impossible—what led observers to call the fall of the Berlin Wall and Soviet Communism, or the South African elections of 1994, "miracles." At such moments whole communities are capable of acts of self-transcendence. Some are able to subordinate their narrow self-interests, for a time, to the society's greater good. In such times, it is the vision of God's domination-free order that prevents us from acquiescing to unworthy visions, or accepting political compromises as anything more than temporary pauses on the path to fuller justice.[4]

2. JESUS' THIRD WAY AS NONVIOLENT-ACTIVE-RESISTANCE

Many, otherwise, devout Christians simply dismiss Jesus' teachings about nonviolence out of hand as impractical idealism. "Turn the other cheek" has come to imply a passive, doormat-like quality that has made the Christian way seem cowardly and complicit in the face of injustice. "Resist not evil" seems to break the back of all opposition to evil and to counsel submission. "Going the second mile" has become a platitude meaning nothing more than "extend yourself," and appears to encourage collaboration with the oppressor. Jesus' teaching, viewed this way, is impractical, masochistic, and even suicidal—creating an invitation to bullies and spouse-batterers to wipe up the floor with their supine Christian victims.

In actuality, Jesus never displayed that kind of passivity. Whatever the source of the misunderstanding, such distortions are clearly neither in Jesus nor his teachings. In context, the following statement by Jesus is one of the most revolutionary political statements ever uttered:[5]

> You have heard that it was said, "An eye for an eye and a tooth for a tooth." But I say to you, Do not resist an evildoer. But if anyone strikes you on the right cheek, turn the other also; and if anyone wants to sue you and take your coat, give your cloak as well; and if anyone forces you to go one mile, go also the second mile (Matt. 5: 38-41; see also Luke 6:29).

The traditional interpretation of "do not resist an evildoer" has been nonresistance to evil—an odd conclusion, given the fact that on every occasion Jesus himself resisted evil with every fiber of his being. Actually, the gospel does not teach nonresistance to evil. Jesus counsels resistance, but without violence. The Greek word translated "resist" in Matt. 5: 39 is *antistenai*, meaning literally to stand (*stenai*) against (*anti*)[6]. In short, it means to resist violently, to revolt or rebel, to engage in an armed insurrection.[7]

A proper translation of Jesus' teaching would then be, "Do not strike back at evil in kind. Do not give blow for blow. Do not retaliate against violence with violence." Jesus was no less committed to opposing evil than the anti-Roman resistance fighters. The only difference was over the means to be used. The issue was *how*—not whether—one should fight evil. There are three general responses to evil: (1) passivity, (2) violent opposition, and (3) the third way of militant nonviolence articulated by Jesus. Human evolution has conditioned us for only the first two of these responses: fight or flight.[8]

Neither of the invidious alternatives of flight/fight is what Jesus is proposing. It is important to be clear about this point before going on: *Jesus abhors both passivity and violence as responses to evil.* His is a third alternative not even touched by these options. *Antistenai* may be translated variously as "Do not take up arms against evil," "Do not react reflexively to evil," "Do not let evil dictate the terms of your opposition."[9]

Today it can be drawn on the cumulative historical experience of nonviolent social struggle over the centuries and employ newer tools for political and social analysis. But the spirit, the thrust, the surge for creative transformation, which is the ultimate principle of the universe, is the same for those who see it incarnated in Jesus. Freed from literalistic legalism, his teaching reads like a practical manual for empowering the powerless to seize the initiative, even in situations impervious to change. It seems almost as if his teaching has only now, in this generation, become an inescapable task and practical necessity.[10]

3. RELIGIO-POLITICAL SETTING OF MYANMAR

Long centuries of Buddhist teaching have led the Burman to ignore God; he does not retain Him in his thoughts, and consequently the Christian message has not attracted him.[11]

This is the common sense of the missionaries who claimed to be the bringers of the gospel to the land where Buddhism had significantly woven in the cultural life of the people along the course of history. Tradition dates the construction of the golden pagoda (*Shwedagon*) back to the sixth century B.C. Hence, the people could not think of their national identity apart from the religion they professed, for it is Buddhism that wielded the Burmese together, and it is the idea of nationhood that owed its inception to this religion.

This has been true since the beginning of the first Burmese kingdom, when Shin Arahan, the first Mon Buddhist monk brought the southern school of Buddhism via Srilanka, and could convince the Burmese conqueror King Anawratha (1044-1077) of the Pagan dynasty (the first Burmese monarchy) to adopt Theravada Buddhism as a state religion.[12]

As a religion, it has to be domesticated itself in the corpus of history and formed the unique whole in the cultural life of the people. Hence, the people come to experience the faith that liberated and enables them to face the struggle against the illusive desires that cause forced poverty. As a metacosmic religion,[13] it can really give value and hope, an eschatological hope in the form of *nirvana*, to the people who from time immemorial practiced the cosmic religion. This liberating dimension of

Buddhism can also be discerned in the progressive revelation perceived during the hard periods when Burma had fallen under foreign dominations from time to time. It is obvious that the liberating-transformative dimension of the religion for the oppressed poor in these oppressive situations had surfaced in the form of religious-nationalism, out of which born the liberation movements led by the monks who represent monastic poverty as the protest against mammon.

"Politic is one of the crucial factors in the revival of Buddhism in Burma can hardly be denied," assessed Dr. U Hla Bu, chairperson of Buddhism studies.[14] And as observed by Aloysius Pieris, it is messianically political, scripturally endorsed and spiritually inspired by the Maitreya cult—the eschatological expectation of a just social order which gives birth to about twenty revolts from 1838 to 1928, initially aimed at Burmese kings and later on directed toward the colonial successors.[15]

It is also true when the second wave of revolutions came during the second exile in Burma under the so-called socialist regime inaugurated by the military coup by General Newin in 1962, which had come to an end with the people's uprising in 1988, in which monks also played a vital part. The liberatingtransformative dimension of Buddhism can be discerned again in the current wave of uprising, centering on the monasteries conducted in solidarity with the oppressed poor who are suffering under the twenty one year long present military regime, which has been an extension of the military dictatorship since 1988.[16]

4. APPLYING JESUS' THIRD WAY IN MYANMAR.

4.1. The Meaning of Love

The first suggestion of the primacy of love in biblical ethics is found in Leviticus 19:18 RSV: "You shall not take vengeance or bear any grudge against the sons of your own people, but you shall love your neighbor as yourself: I am the Lord." Jesus said that the whole of Old Testament morality rested upon the love for God and the love for neighbor. Paul said that the love of one's neighbor was the fulfillment of the law (Gal. 5: 14) and in the famous "love chapter" (1Cor. 13) love is set forth as the supreme Christian virtue.[17]

Love is inseparably bound up with the name of Jesus Christ as the revelation of God. He is the only definition of love. But again it would be a complete misunderstanding if we were to derive a general definition of love from our view of Jesus Christ and of His deed and His suffering. Love is not what He *does* and what He *suffers*, but it is what *He* does and what *He* suffers.[18] The love with which man loves God and his neighbor is the love of God and no other; for there is no other love that is free or independent from the love of God. Loving God is simply the other aspect of being loved by God. Being loved by God implies loving God; the two do not stand separately side by side.[19] Christian love, therefore, is not desire. It is giving love— nonreciprocal, neighbor-regarding—where "neighbor" means "everybody," even an enemy (Luke 6:32-35).[20]

When applied to ethics love has the following characteristics:[21]
1) Love is a positive feeling tone
2) Love is a policy to seek the good for others
3) Love as an ethical attitude is love that comes to concrete expression
4) Love is full of grace
5) Love is universal

4.2. Forgiveness and Reconciliation
The call to follow Christ always means, as Bonhoeffer insisted, a

call to share the work of forgiving men their sins and forgiveness is the Christ-like suffering which it is the Christian's duty to bear.[22] In fact, the goal of forgiveness is always reconciliation.[23] First and foremost, it should be realized that God has taken the initiative to reconcile us, both to God and to each other. The reconciliation to God and human beings envisioned in narrative Christus Victor is in no way it based on tolerance and mutual acceptance.[24] Past complicity with the Domination System needs to be acknowledged. Old enmities must be healed, for unsolved hatreds can lead to acts of revenge by those newly empowered, so that the old system of domination is continued in the new.[25] Reconciliation requires that one and the other person from whom one have been separated by enmity, mutually forgive each other and walk into a common future together.[26] Moreover, reconciliation means, finally, reestablishing love between two or more estranged parties.[27]

4.3. Loving Our Enemies

Love of enemies is the recognition that the enemy, too, is a child of God. The enemy too believes he or she is in the right, and fears others because they represent a threat against his or her values, lifestyle, or affluence. When they demonize their enemies, calling them names and identifying them with absolute evil, they deny that their enemies have that of God within them that make transformation possible. Instead, they play God. They write their enemies out of the Book of Life. They conclude that their enemy has drifted beyond the redemptive hand of God.[28]

Walter Wink insists, "I submit that the ultimate religious question today is no longer the Reformation's 'How can I find a gracious God?' It is instead, 'How can I find God in my enemy?' What guilt was for Luther, the enemy has become for us: the goad that can drive us to God. What has formerly been a purely private affair—justification by faith through grace—has now, in our age, grown to embrace the world. As John Stoner comments, we can no more save ourselves from our enemies that we can save ourselves from sin, but God's amazing grace offers to save us from both. There is, in fact, no other way to God for our time but through the enemy, for loving the enemy has become the key both to human survival in the age of terror and to personal transformation."[29]

Faith in God, then, means believing that anyone can be transformed, regardless of the past. Love of enemies is trusting God for the miracle of divine forgiveness. If God can forgive, redeem, and transform, it must also be believed that God can work such wonders with anyone. It is seeing one's oppressors through the prism of the Reign of God—not only as they now are, but also as what they can become: transformed by the power of God.[30]

4.4. Constructive Negotiation

In Myanmar, Dr. Tun Aung Chang said that there is no right and wrong but only negotiation.[31] I assume that it includes decreasing human dignity in Myanmar. Through that negotiation, the Law has no value and one those who have authority can do everything he/she wishes, even if it is harmful for those who are innocent. Therefore, everyone who does not take the foundation of this negotiation from love, will most certainly have a destructive negotiation. Christians in Myanmar do need to take off any boundaries of injustice, lawlessness, guilty, and separation from love by constructive negotiation. Actually, it is not only the duty of the Christians but all the citizens. The Christians must first show what Jesus has shown with his self-sacrificed life for seeking the truth.

Myanmar is going to participate in its elections in 2010. Here, both the military regime, those who participate in this, and all the citizens need to have constructive negotiations. If the military regime will be seen as absolutely wrong, it will also be wrong. Even if all oppose their evil spirit, love must be shown as forgiveness upon them. Totally, they are opposed; the nonviolent movement will be, as Gandhi distinguished, the nonviolence of the weak, which uses harassment to break the opponent.[32] To be, which the Christians share, love in action as the nonviolence of the strong, the people must strive to make the military regime's good by freeing them from oppressive actions. Thence, our negotiation will be a constructive.

CONCLUSION

Human beings are created as the image of God and each has his/her dignity. We must realize that even our enemies have human dignity. All are precious to God for participating as a tool for building peaceful community. In Myanmar, while Aung San Suu Kyi is being loved, General Than Shwe should not be ignored. It is the responsiblility of every citizen that the future not happen like the *Eight-Eight-Eighty Eight revolution* is the responsibility. The nonviolent movement has to be the nonviolence of the strong. The citizens must be trained as Martin L. King, Jr. had done fifty years ago. As a saying "the end justifies the means," love in action should be both our means and our end. While nonviolent resistance can be the most difficult, it can also be acceptable and practicable for everyone. It also is the central model, which the conditions of Myanmar' demand, in the areas of conducting mission. It may cost many lives, but if we establish our foundation in love, it will someday be a flower which blooms full of sweet smell, beauty and bright for everyone. Thence, everyone will realize that Myanmar is a peaceful community and a fruitful field in the world.

END NOTES

1. Hau Sian Suan is from Myanmar and a third year M.Div Student at Myanmar Institute of Theology, Yangon, Myanmar.

2. Walter Wink, *When The Powers Fall: Reconciliation In The Healing of Nations* (Minneapolis: Fortress Press, 1998), 9. See also Walter Wink, Engaging the Powers: Discernment and Resistance in a World of Domination (Minneapolis: Fortress Press, 1992), chap. 9.

3. Ibid, 10.

4. Ibid, 11-12.

5. Walter Wink, *The Powers That Be: Theology for A New Millennium* (New York: Doubleday, 1998), 98.

6. Ibid, 99.

7. Ibid, 100.

8. Walter Wink, "Jesus' Third Way" in *Transforming Violence: Linking Local and Global Peacemaking*, edited by Robert Herr and Judy Zimmerman Herr (Scottdale: Herald Press, 1998), 35.

9. Ibid, 35-36.

10. Ibid, 46-47.

11. Saw Hlaing Bwa, "Mission: Christio-Praxis in Myanmar" in Missio Dei, Vol. 2 (February, 2008), 7. See *Wesleyan Methodist Missionary Society Report* (1926), quoted in Alexander Mcleish, Christian Progress In Burmar, London: World Dominion Press, 1929, 28.

12. Ibid, 7-8.

13. Metacosmic religion defines its soteriology in terms of a metacosmic "beyond" capable of being internalized as the salvific "within" of the human person, either through the agapeic path of redeeming love or through the Gnostic way of liberating knowledge.

14. Ibid, 9. See Hla Bu, "The Nature of Buddhist Resurgence in Burma," in: *South East Asia Journal of Theology III*, (1/1960), 27.

15. Ibid, 9. See Aloysius Pieris, *An Asian Theology of Liberation* (Edinburgh: T&T Clark, 1998), 105.

16. Ibid, 10.

17. Bernard L. Ramm, *The Right, The Good & The Happy* (Waco: Word Books, 1971), 44.

18. Dietrich Bonhoeffer, *Ethics*, First Touchstone Edition (New York: Touchstone Rockefeller Center, 1995), 54.

19. Ibid, 56.

20. Joseph Fletcher, *Situation Ethics: The New Morality* (Louisville: Westminster John Knox Press, 1966), 79.

21. *The Right, The Good & The Happy*, 45.

22. Dietrich Bonhoeffer, *The Cost of Discipleship* (New York: Macmillan Company, 1963), 100.

23. *When The Powers Fall: Reconciliation in the Healing of Nations*, 16.

24. J. Denny Weaver, *The Nonviolent Atonement* (Grand Rapids: W.B. Eerdmans Publishing Company, 2001), 216. In narrative Christus Victor, without transformation of life, without a cessation of oppressive activity and a beginning of confrontation of oppression, there is no reconciliation.

25. *When The Powers Fall: Reconciliation in the Healing of Nations*, 13.

26. Ibid, 14.

27. Ibid, 16.

28. Walter Wink, *Jesus and Nonviolence: A Third Way* (Minneapolis: Fortress Press, 2003), 59.

29. Ibid, 59-60.

30. Ibid, 68-69.

31. Lecture Notes from Theology of Mission by Rev. Dr. Cung Lian Hup at Soward Hall, MIT on September 7, 2009.

32. *Jesus and Nonviolence: A Third Way*, 64.

BIBLIOGRAPHY

Bonhoeffer, Dietrich. *Ethics*, First Touchstone Edition. New York: TouchstoneRockefeller Center, 1995.

--------- *The Cost of Discipleship*. New York: Macmillan Company, 1963.

Fletcher, Joseph. *Situation Ethics: The New Morality*. Louisville: Westminster John Knox Press, 1966.

Herr, Robert and Judy Zimmerman Herr, editors. *Transforming Violence*. Scottdale: Herald Press, 1998.

L. Ramm, Bernard. *The Right, The Good & The Happy*. Waco: Word Books, 1971.

Missio Dei, Volume 2. MIT: February, 2008.

Weaver, J. Denny. *The Nonviolent Atonement*. Grand Rapids: W.B. Eerdmans Publishing Company, 2001.

Wink, Walter. *Jesus and Nonviolence: A Third Way*. Minneapolis: Fortress Press, 2003.

---------*The Powers That Be: Theology for A New Millennium*. New York: Doubleday, 1998.

---------*When The Powers Fall: Reconciliation In The Healing of Nations*. Minneapolis: Fortress Press, 1998.

6

Ecumenism: Moving Toward a Multi-Faceted Global Conversation

Mission and Unity: Ecclesiology and Mission

Jamie Lynn Hollis[1]

As Christians around the world anticipate and prepare for the coming centennial celebration of Edinburgh's 1910 World Missionary Conference, study groups and individuals consider what it means for the church to be visibly united and what that has to do with mission. We consider what it means for the "whole church to take the whole Gospel to the whole world," as the Lausanne Congress on World Evangelization affirmed in 1974.[2] We look back on the last 100 years, both asking for forgiveness and celebrating God's work, and, in response, Jacques Matthey calls us to "move towards a vision for mission in the future."[3]

The issue of mission and unity was the very concern that gave birth to the 1910 conference in Edinburgh. At that time, this conference was made up of representatives from missionary societies rather than representatives from churches or denominations.[4] But, in the last hundred years, churches and denominations have slowly replaced mission agencies in this ongoing conversation.[5] Because of their nature, mission agencies tend to be more adept and practiced (though not perfect) at crossing cultural and linguistic divides than denominational agencies, which tend to work, rather, at crossing doctrinal and (obviously) denominational divides. These differences are shaping this ongoing conversation. I would like to suggest something that might seem obvious, but I do so because it seems to be easily overlooked in conversation and practice today: the word 'ecumenical' not only means working across denominational divides, as is commonly assumed, but also includes the concept of working together, united across other divides that exist in the global church. The visibly united church is not only made up of various denominations working together, but also of Christians of various cultures and languages. We must, therefore, through the grace of God, work across and through, not only denominations, but also cultures, languages, contexts, political lines, economic divides, disciplines, strengths, weaknesses and quirks. What does this fuller understanding of ecumenism bring to the belief that the *whole church* is called to take the *whole gospel* to the *whole world?*

Prior to the 1910 conference, missionaries began to recognize that the competition, conflict and divisions occurring between missionaries and agencies working in the same and neighboring regions and from different denominational backgrounds undermined the credibility of that to which they wanted to witness: the love of Christ. These conflicts were addressed at local and regional levels, often resulting in 'comity agreements,' but there was still a felt need for a global partnership in Christian mission. At the same time, missionaries often found themselves developing close relationships with fellow Christians across these same denominational lines, despite their differences. Such relationships across perceived divides were unlikely to develop in first-culture settings, but, in foreign territory, that which they had in common often drew these Christians together. It was in this context that Fairley Daly, the Secretary of the Livingstonia Mission Committee, wrote to Robert Speer, Secretary of the Presbyterian Board of Foreign Missions in New York, to suggest the planning of a major missionary conference to follow up on the Ecumenical Mission Conference of 1900.[6] While the 1900 conference was a conference on the mobilization of mission, the 1910 conference was to be a consultation on mission strategy.

The Edinburgh 1910 conference resulted in nine published volumes, one of which is *Report of Commission VIII: Co-operation and the Promotion of Unity*.[7] In this document, contributors assessed that in order for the establishment of Christ's one Church in 'non-Christian lands'—the "achievement of the ultimate and highest end of all missionary work"—"real unity must be attained."[8] And yet doctrinal and structural differences between organizations and denominations were intentionally avoided with the hope that they might prevent theological conflict. In spite of this deliberate avoidance, some delegates, especially from China, expressed the hope that the oneness of the church might be made more apparent in the future.[9]

At the 1951 Rolle meeting of the Central Committee of the World Council of Churches, participants articulated that everything that relates to the whole task given by God, who is love, to the whole Church must express unity in every facet of its existence. They believed that the word 'ecumenical' must be used to cover issues of both *unity* and *mission* and in the context of the *whole world*.[10] In 1982, the World Council of Churches took this position a step further, expressing the inextricable nature of the church's missionary calling with visible Christian unity, between evangelization and ecumenism.[11] They pointed to evangelization as the "test of our ecumenical vocation."[12] While evangelization most certainly is the test of our ecumenical vocation, it is ironic that this same concern was also the fuel that pushed the movement into being, and it is frustrating that we are still addressing this same issue one hundred years later.

It was in the crossing of cultures and languages that the modern ecumenical movement was born, and to these roots we must return if we hope to explore what it means to evangelize as a visibly united church, wholly representing One God Who is Three, holding our differences in tension and in love.

WHOLE CHURCH

At a recent conference that addressed some of the study themes for the coming centennial, Cecil M. Robeck, Jr. presented a paper in which he underscores that, in response to Jesus' prayer for unity among his disciples, God gifted the church with ecumenism.[13] Our call is not to create unity, but, rather, as Ephesians 4.3 admonishes, to maintain the unity that has already been given to us.[14] Unity implies wholeness, or, as Princeton University's lexical database, WordNet, describes in one of three possible definitions, is "an undivided or unbroken completeness or totality with nothing wanting."[15] In a united church every language is represented, and every culture is recognized—each people engages and learns from the others. Jacques Matthey reminds us in "Evangelism, Still the Enduring Test of Our Ecumenical — and Missionary Calling" that Christ died, according to Ephesians and Colossians, "to make Jews and the gentile nations into one, and to make the church one and multi-racial."[16] The whole church is a global, multi-ethnic, multi-cultured, multi-lingual church.

According to a more recent statement of faith pointed to by the Lausanne Theology Working Group, the church "exists to worship and glorify God for all eternity and is commissioned by Christ and empowered by the Holy Spirit to participate in the transforming mission of God within history."[17] David J. Bosch understands ecclesiology, ecumenism and mission as woven together and states that "mission is *missio Dei* which seeks to subsume into itself the *missiones ecclesiae*, the missionary programs of the church."[18] The church does not "undertake" mission. Rather, the *missio Dei* constitutes the church.[19] Only insofar as the church participates in God's mission does the church exist.[20] This multi-faceted church is made of and for God's activity in and sending into the whole world with the whole gospel.

WHOLE GOSPEL

A whole understanding of the gospel must include understandings of the contextualized gospel from other nations and cultures. Obviously, we, as individual Christians, cannot hope to comprehend the *whole* gospel in this lifetime. But every culture does need to be engaged in taking their contextualization of the gospel to other cultures in the world and also in the receiving of this same good news as articulated by cultures other than their own. Again, while each locality cannot send or receive delegates from the world over, there must be an intentional sending and receiving of Christians between cultures. This does not mean that we should export the good news as we know it from Elkhart, Indiana, in the United States, to the Arab village of I'blin, in the Galilee region of Israel, for mass consumption or that the Christians of I'blin should export their understanding of the gospel for those of us living in Elkhart to absorb uncritically. But the gospel, as it is understood in I'blin, Elkhart and other places from around the world must be exchanged with other cultures in order for the whole church to have a glimpse of the whole gospel. These contextualized understandings of the gospel shed light on experiences of the church in other localities, and we would all benefit in the broadening of our understanding of what it means to be "church" in cultures other than those we have already experienced. Christians as individuals often understand themselves in terms of their denomination. But, perhaps at a more basic level, they also understand themselves through their physical and cultural locations.

When we speak of ecumenism, we must not only mean cooperation and learning among denominations, but also, and maybe especially, among cultures and peoples living in particular settings. This understanding of ecumenism calls for not only church and denominational leaders to be in conversation, but for these leaders to also work and walk hand-in-hand with missionaries and those skilled at crossing linguistic and cultural borders toward a visible realization of the *whole church* bringing the *whole gospel*.

Matthias Wenk's definition of the church's mission, as expressed at a recent conference, is to exist as "the visible demonstration of God's healing and restoring work in this world."[21] Because Christ is the visible manifestation of God's healing work and the restoration of this world, we can then understand the church as the continuation of Christ's ministry.[22] The World Council of Churches affirms that healing "includes the transformation of life made possible by crossing cultural and religious boundaries."[23] Visible unity, then, is the living out of the gospel of healing and restoration and in partnership—an act of healing and restoration itself—with Christians of other cultures from around the world. This act of healing is not only then linked to crossing cultural boundaries, but also to the mission of the church, and, again, adds to our understanding of *wholeness*. The *whole gospel* is what is presented when the transformed church, visibly united across cultural and religious boundaries, demonstrates God's healing and restoring work. What, then, might we mean by *whole world?*

Whole World

The Commission on World Mission and Evangelism of the World Council of Churches recognized in 1964 that the missionary movement involved Christians "in all six continents and in all lands."[24] And while Ralph D. Winter, co-founder of the American Society of Missiology, would argue that this mission should not just be *in*, but also *between* lands, the commission did recognize the importance of the involvement of *all* Christians in *all* locations.[25] Bosch states that "mission in unity means an end to the distinction between 'sending' and 'receiving' churches."[26] And in 1968, an American missionary serving in Cost Rica declared that "every Christian in every church throughout the world *is equally obligated* to spread the gospel to the entire world either by going or by giving."[27]

Lesslie Newbigin argued in 1961 that the unity we desire to make visible, and the unity Christ prayed for, is for the sake of the world, "which God made and loves and for which He sent His Son."[28] Pain and poverty, suffering and oppression all exist in this world. And yet we are called, as the *whole church* to bring the *whole gospel* to the *whole world*. How can the world be *whole* when suffering exists? When the united church demonstrates God's healing work we visibly attest to the renewing wholeness of the world. The *whole world* is the world that God is in the process of healing—human and creation, Christian and non-Christian alike. The in-the-process-of-being-restored-world can only receive the gospel if it is a whole-healing-restoring-gospel.

It will take many diverse articulations in order for us to have a glimpse of this whole gospel. Let us continue to listen and reach across the many tangible and intangible divides as we once again assess and discover what it means to be the *whole church* called to bring the *whole gospel* to the *whole world*.

END NOTES

1. Jamie Lynn Hollis is from the United States and a Master of Divinity student at Associated Mennonite Biblical Seminary. She recently completed an internship with Mennonite Mission Network in Israel and has prior experience in Kyrgyzstan. Jamie is also the assistant to the Mission Studies Center in Elkhart, Indiana.

2. John Stott, *Lausanne Covenant* (Lausanne, Switzerland: Lausanne Congress on World Evangelization, 1974), http://www.lausanne.org/covenant (accessed December 13, 2009).

3. Jacques Matthey, "'I am Gentle and Humble in Heart' (Matthew 11.29): Mission and Power" (paper presented at the European Pentecostal Charismatic Research Association Conference, Oxford, UK: Oxford Centre for Mission Studies, August 12-15, 2009), 1, http://www.edinburgh2010.org/fileadmin/files/edinburgh2010/files/pdf/jacques_matthey.pdf (accessed December 9, 2009).

4. Laszlo Gonda et al., "Towards Common Witness to Christ Today: Mission and the Visible Unity of the Church" (study paper on Theme 8 of the Edinburgh 2010 Study Process, submitted by the Commission on World Mission and Evangelism, World Council of Churches, September 2009), 2, http://www.edinburgh2010.org/en/studythemes/1-foundations-for-mission/blog.html?tx_wecdiscussion%5Bsingle%5D=1479 (accessed December 9, 2009).

5. See Ralph D. Winter, "The Legacy of Edinburgh, 1910" in *The Unfolding Drama of the Christian Movement* (Pasadena,

California: Institute of International Studies, 1979) http://
www.edinburgh2010.org/fileadmin/files/edinburgh2010/
files/pdf/Ralph%20Winter%20-%20Edinburgh%201910.
pdf (accessed December 9, 2009).

6. Kenneth R. Ross, *Edinburgh 2010: Springboard for Mission*
(Pasadena, California: William Carey International
University Press, 2009), 4.

7. World Missionary Conference 1910: Report of
Commission VIII: Co-operation and the Promotion
of Unity (Edinburgh and London: Oliphant,
Anderson and Ferrier), http://www.archive.org/stream/
reportofcommissi08worluoft#page/n5/mode/2up (accessed
December 12, 2009).

8. Ibid., 5.

9. Ross, *Edinburgh 2010: Springboard for Mission*, 11.

10. World Council of Churches, Minutes and Reports of
the Fourth Meeting of the Central Committee (Rolle,
Switzerland: August 4-11, 1951), 65, quoted by Gonda et
al., "Towards Common Witness to Christ Today," 3.

11. World Council of Churches, "Mission and Evangelism:
An Ecumenical Affirmation" (Geneva, Switzerland: World
Council of Churches, 1982), http://www.religion-online.
org/showchapter.asp?title=1573&C=1525 (accessed
December 13, 2009).

12. Philip Potter (speech to the Roman Catholic Synod of
Bishops, Rome: 1974), quoted by World Council of Churches,
"Mission and Evangelism: An Ecumenical Affirmation."

13. Cecil M. Robeck Jr., "Christian Unity and Pentecostal Mission: A Contradiction?" (paper presented at the European Pentecostal Charismatic Research Association Conference, Oxford, UK: Oxford Centre for Mission Studies, August 12-15, 2009), 7, http://www. edinburgh2010.org/fileadmin/files/edinburgh2010/files/ pdf/cecil_robeck.pdf (accessed December 9, 2009).

14. Ibid., 7n13.

15. WordNet, s.v. "Unity" (Princeton University, 2009), http:// wordnetweb.princeton.edu/perl/webwn?s=unity (accessed December 14, 2009).

16. Jacques Matthey, "Evangelism, Still the Enduring Test of our Ecumenical — and Missionary Calling," International Review of Mission 96, no. 382-383 (2007): 367.

17. Tear Fund Statement of Faith (2007), quoted by Lausanne Theology Working Group, "The Whole Church: Reflections of the Lausanne Theology Working Group" (reflections from meeting: Panama, January 26-30, 2009), 2, http://www.edinburgh2010.org/fileadmin/files/ edinburgh2010/files/pdf/TWG09Panama-Statement-CW. pdf (accessed December 9, 2009).

18. David J. Bosch, *Transforming Mission: Paradigm Shifts in Theology of Mission* (Maryknoll, New York: Orbis Books, 1991), 519.

19. Ibid.

20. Gonda et al., "Towards Common Witness to Christ Today," 10.

21. Matthias Wenk, "Reconciliation and Renunciation of Status as God's Final Aim for Humanity: New Testament Thoughts on the Church's Mission and Unity" (paper presented at the European Pentecostal Charismatic Research Association Conference, Oxford, UK: Oxford Centre for Mission Studies, August 12-15, 2009), 1, http:// www. edinburgh2010.org/fileadmin/files/edinburgh2010/ files/pdf/matthias_wenk.pdf (accessed December 9, 2009).

22. Ibid., 1-2.

23. Turid Karlssen Seim, *The Double Message: Patterns of Gender in Luke-Acts* (Edinburgh: T&T Clark, 1994), 57, quoted by Gonda et al., "Towards Common Witness to Christ Today," 15.

24. World Council of Churches, "The Message of the Commission on World Mission and Evangelism of the World Council of Churches," Ecumenical Review 16, no. 3 (April 1964): 305.

25. Winter, "The Legacy of Edinburgh, 1910," 303.

26. Bosch, *Transforming Mission*, 465.

27. David Kensinger, "Integrating National Missions into our World Evangelization Program" (unpublished address to Assemblies of God Missionaries, Springfield, Missouri: Assemblies of God World Mission Archives, 1968), quoted by DeLonn Rance, "The Church in Latin America: Coming Together in Mission," (paper presented at the European Pentecostal Charismatic Research Association Conference, Oxford, UK: Oxford Centre for Mission Studies, August 13, 2009), 15, http://www.edinburgh2010.

org/fileadmin/files/edinburgh2010/files/pdf/delonn_ rance.
pdf (accessed December 9, 2009).

28. Lesslie Newbigin, *Is Christ Divided? A Plea for Christian
Unity in a Revolutionary Age* (Grand Rapids, Michigan:
William B. Eerdmans Publishing Company, 1961), 22.

SELECTED BIBLIOGRAPHY

Bosch, David J. *Transforming Mission: Paradigm Shifts in Theology
of Mission.* Maryknoll, New York: Orbis Books, 1991.

Cooney, Monica. "Towards Common Witness: A Call to
Adopt Responsible Relationships in Mission and to Avoid
Proselytism." *International Review of Mission* 85, no. 337
(April 1996): 283-289.

Enose, Beno A. "Edinburgh 2010: A Stepping Stone for
Indian Ecumenical Unity and Christian Leadership."
Tamil Nadu, India. http://www.edinburgh2010.org/en/
study-themes/1-foundationsfor- mission/blog.html?tx_
wecdiscussion%5Bsingle%5D=1536 (accessed December
9, 2009).

Gonda, Laszlo, Ron Wallace, Jooseop Keum, Dimitra
Koukoura, and Raymond Pfister. "Towards Common
Witness to Christ Today: Mission and the Visible Unity of
the Church." Study Paper on Theme 8 of the Edinburgh
2010 Study Process. Submitted by the Commission
on World Mission and Evangelism, World Council of
Churches, September 2009. http://www.edinburgh2010.
org/en/study-themes/1-foundations-for-mission/blog.
html?tx_wecdiscussion%5Bsingle%5D=14 7 9 (accessed
December 9, 2009).

Guder, Darrell L. ed. *Missional Church: A Vision for the Sending of the Church in North America*. Grand Rapids, Michigan: William B. Eerdmans Publishing Company, 1998.

Harfst, Pfarrerin Ursula. "Between Power and Powerlessness: A Personal Journey with Migrant Christians." Paper presented, European Pentecostal Charismatic Research Association Conference, Oxford, UK: Oxford Centre for Mission Studies, August 12-15, 2009. http://www. edinburgh2010.org/fileadmin/files/edinburgh2010/files/ pdf/ursula_harfst.pdf (accessed December 9, 2009).

Hocken, Peter. "Two Movements of the Holy Spirit of the 20th Century: Can They Come Together After 100 Years? The Pentecostal-Charismatic Contribution to Christian Unity." Paper presented, European Pentecostal Charismatic Research Association Conference, Oxford, UK: Oxford Centre for Mission Studies, August 14, 2009. http://www. edinburgh2010.org/fileadmin/files/edinburgh2010/files/ pdf/peter_hocken.pdf (accessed December 9, 2009).

Hoekendijk, Johannes. *The Church Inside Out*. Edited by L.A. Hoedemaker and Pieter Tijmes. Translated by Isaac C. Rottenberg. Philadelphia, Pennsylvania: The Westminster Press, 1966. First published in Dutch under the title De Derk Binnenste Buiten. Amsterdam: W. Ten Have, 1964.

-------- *Horizons of Hope*. Lecture delivered, Atlanta, Georgia: Candler School of Theology, Emory University, January 1970. Published in Nashville, Tennessee: Tidings, 1970.

Kerr, David A. and Kenneth R. Ross, eds. *Edinburgh 2010: Mission Then and Now*. Pasadena, California: William Carey International University Press, 2009.

Lausanne Theology Working Group. "The Whole Church: Reflections of the Lausanne Theology Working Group." Reflections, meeting, Panama, January 26-30, 2009. http:// www.edinburgh2010.org/fileadmin/files/edinburgh2010/ files/pdf/TWG09Panama-Statement-CW.pdf (accessed December 9, 2009).

Matthey, Jacques. "Evangelism, Still the Enduring Test of our Ecumenical — and Missionary Calling." International Review of Mission 96, no. 382-383 (2007): 355-367.

-------- "'I am Gentle and Humble in Heart' (Matthew 11.29): Mission and Power." Paper presented, European Pentecostal Charismatic Research Association Conference, Oxford, UK: Oxford Centre for Mission Studies, August 12-15, 2009. http://www.edinburgh2010.org/fileadmin/files/ edinburgh2010/files/pdf/jacques_matthey.pdf (accessed December 9, 2009).

Newbigin, Lesslie. Is Christ Divided? A Plea for Christian Unity in a Revolutionary Age. Grand Rapids, Michigan: William B. Eerdmans Publishing Company, 1961.

Papathanasiou, Athanasios N. "Is Mission a Consequence of the Catholicity of the Church? An Orthodox Perspective." International Review of Mission 90, no. 359 (October 2001): 409-416.

Rance, DeLonn. "The Church in Latin America: Coming Together in Mission." Paper presented, European Pentecostal Charismatic Research Association Conference, Oxford, UK: Oxford Centre for Mission Studies, August 13, 2009. http:// www.edinburgh2010.org/fileadmin/files/ edinburgh2010/ files/pdf/delonn_rance.pdf (accessed December 9, 2009).

Robeck Jr., Cecil M. "Christian Unity and Pentecostal
Mission: A Contradiction?" Paper presented, European
Pentecostal Charismatic Research Association Conference,
Oxford, UK: Oxford Centre for Mission Studies, August
12-15, 2009. http://www.edinburgh2010.org/fileadmin/
files/ edinburgh2010/files/pdf/cecil_robeck.pdf (accessed
December 9, 2009).

Ross, Kenneth R. *Edinburgh 2010: Springboard for Mission.*
Pasadena, California: William Carey International
University Press, 2009.

Stanley, Brian. *The World Missionary Conference, Edinburgh
1910.* Grand Rapids, Michigan: William B. Eerdmans
Publishing Company, 2009.

Stromberg, Jean S. "Ecumenical Affirmation on Mission and
Evangelism: A Review." *International Review of Mission* 90,
no. 358 (July 2001): 243-252.

John Stott. Lausanne Covenant. Lausanne, Switzerland:
Lausanne Congress on World Evangelization, 1974. http://
www.lausanne.org/covenant (accessed December 13, 2009).

Warrington, Keith. "Cracked or Broken: Pentecostal Unity."
Paper presented, European Pentecostal Charismatic Research
Association Conference, Oxford, UK: Oxford Centre
for Mission Studies, August 12-15, 2009. http://www.
edinburgh2010.org/fileadmin/files/edinburgh2010/files/pdf/
keith_warrington.pdf (accessed December 9, 2009).

Wenk, Matthias. "Reconciliation and Renunciation of Status as
God's Final Aim for Humanity: New Testament Thoughts
on the Church's Mission and Unity." Paper presented,

European Pentecostal Charismatic Research Association Conference, Oxford, UK: Oxford Centre for Mission Studies, August 12-15, 2009. http://www.edinburgh2010. org/fileadmin/files/edinburgh2010/files/pdf/matthias_ wenk.pdf (accessed December 9, 2009).

Winter, Ralph D. "The Legacy of Edinburgh, 1910." In *The Unfolding Drama of the Christian Movement.* Pasadena, California: Institute of International Studies, 1979. http:// www.edinburgh2010.org/fileadmin/files/edinburgh2010/ files/pdf/Ralph%20Winter%20-%20Edinburgh%201910. pdf (accessed December 9, 2009).

World Council of Churches. "The Message of the Commission on World Mission and Evangelism of the World Council of Churches." *Ecumenical Review* 16, no. 3 (April 1964): 304-323.

--------"Mission and Evangelism: An Ecumenical Affirmation." Geneva, Switzerland: World Council of Churches, 1982. http://www.religion-online.org/showchapter. asp?title=1573&C=1525 (accessed December 13, 2009).

--------*Nature and Mission of the Church: A Stage on the Way to a Common Statement,* Faith and Order Paper, no. 198. Geneva, Switzerland: World Council of Churches Publications, 2007.

World Missionary Conference 1910: Report of Commission VIII: Co-operation and the Promotion of Unity. Edinburgh and London: Oliphant, Anderson and Ferrier. http://www. archive.org/stream/ reportofcommissi08worluoft#page/n5/ mode/2up (accessed December 12, 2009).

7

"The Word Became Flesh and Lived Among Us": The Missiological Implications of an Incarnational Christology

Foundations for Mission

Jesse Zink[1]

The first and central fact of Christ's existence on earth is that God "became flesh and lived among us" (John 1:14).[2] This is the miracle of the Incarnation: an omniscient, omnipotent, and all-mighty God voluntarily took human form to love, teach, heal, and save humankind in his ministry, death, and resurrection. It is commonplace in missiology to see the reconciling mission of God in Good Friday's cross and Easter's empty tomb. God loved us and died for us that we might be reconciled both to God and one another and restore the right relationships that existed in Creation. Yet the cross and tomb are impossible without the manger on Christmas. In a similar way in the 21st century, mission must first be preceded by a self-emptying incarnation that creates a new way of being. The Incarnation is the foundation on which mission rests.

In this essay, I seek to draw out the missiological implications of a Christology that places central importance on the Incarnation. I first examine the features of Christ's Incarnation and show how missionaries can emulate these in their mission existence. I then outline several implications of a view of incarnational mission and cite one important way in which humans fall short of Christ's incarnational model. I conclude by asking how truly incarnational contemporary models of mission in the Western world are.

There are three important features of Christ's Incarnation that can shape contemporary mission efforts. First, the Incarnation allowed God to share an existence with humankind. Second, the Incarnation allowed God to share the message of salvation in a culturally-specific and -appropriate way. Third, the Incarnation altered the power dynamics in the divine-human relationship such that God chose to become vulnerable and weak, and, in so doing, more effectively communicated the message of reconciliation.

In Christian cosmology, there is a dividing line between the realm of God and that of human beings. Wherever and however God exists, it is certainly not within the bounds of this earthly realm. God is beyond Creation and therefore beyond our world, which is the result of God's creative act. As humans, we do well to remember that no matter how much knowledge we can have of our own world, there is an entire other realm of which we cannot know in this life.

For centuries, God tried to create a just order by working and speaking through human beings, staying on the divine side of the divide but repeatedly reaching out to the human side in the patriarchs and matriarchs, prophets, judges, and kings. This is the history of the Old Testament. But the fallible and fallen human beings chosen by God always fell short and their work had little lasting impact in restoring the right relationships God yearns for humans to have. The significance of the Incarnation is that God intentionally chose to break down this long-standing barrier between divine and human, to come "to what was his own" (John 1:11), and cross into the world God had created. The result was that God in the form of Jesus Christ lived and walked and existed on this earth with other human beings. It was an entirely new act for God and a stunning one: God dwelt on this earth and shared human existence.

The traditional divide between the divine and human realms also comes with a power differential. The Holy One of Israel is all-mighty and far more powerful than humans can ever imagine. This is clear from repeated references in the Old Testament. For instance, in some of the oldest Hebrew in the Bible, Moses celebrates after the triumph over the Egyptians at the Red Sea: "The Lord is my strength and my might… The Lord is a warrior… Your right hand, O Lord, glorious in power" (Exod. 15:2,3,6).

In the context of this view of God, it is notable that the Incarnation took place in a back-alley stable with a manger for a crib, surrounded not by attendants worthy of such a mighty being but by shepherds and animals. This is the first of many indications in Christ's ministry that God has chosen to shed the power and majesty that is God's alone for a different sort of existence. Christ's life and ministry were marked by a striking degree of vulnerability. Christ was a wandering teacher, traveling from town to town, apparently dependent on the generosity of others for food and shelter. This vulnerability is uniquely encapsulated in the cross, in which Christ willingly chose a degrading death so that humankind might live eternally. It is expressed most fully in the Christ hymn in Philippians: Christ "emptied himself, taking the form of a slave, being born in human likeness…. he humbled himself and became obedient to the point of death" (2:7-8). To use the Greek word for "empty" in this passage, Christ's ministry, beginning at the moment of the Incarnation, is kenotic in that God altered the usual power dynamics between the divine and human realm and submitted to a lesser power. In willingly giving up power, God was able to bring about the reconciliation that is at the core of God's mission.

The result of this decision to share an existence with humans and to be vulnerable is that God was able to share God's message in a particular way that people readily understood. By sharing a common heritage and upbringing and seeking not domination but dependence, Jesus was able to turn everyday occurrences into opportunities to share the good news of the kingdom of God. Thus, a woman going about her daily chores at a well learned about the love of God (John 4:7-42), a people who grew up hearing the Torah recited heard it interpreted in entirely new ways (e.g. Luke 4:16-21), and a beggar by the side of the road was healed and made new (e.g. Mark 10:46-52). Because the message was appropriately enculturated and presented in a graceful rather than domineering way, it was well received and acted upon. None of these life-altering moments would have been possible without the miracle of the Incarnation.

If the foundations of God's mission of reconciliation are found in the Incarnation, our missional efforts must also have similar foundations. In our case, we cannot choose to cross the barrier between divine and human. Yet there are other great barriers in this world based on well-known factors such as wealth, education, race, gender, and more. As a whole, these barriers can be characterized as dividing those who, on the one hand, lead an existence that is relatively secure, who can wake up in the morning and know, for instance, where their next meal is coming from, that they won't be summarily evicted from their housing. and that their children can afford to stay in school; and, on the other hand, those whose existence is not at all secure and who must live in constant fear and uncertainty about how they will be able to react to what the future might bring. The division between secure and insecure cuts right through the middle of countries, even those that have historically been privileged. In the past, mission efforts have often been sent from the secure world to the insecure world, though many people in the world inhabit both sides of the divide at different points in time, sometimes simultaneously.

The three lessons from Christ's Incarnation are applicable in a similar way to our missional efforts across this barrier in our world. Incarnational mission begins in the decision to share an existence with people in a new place and a new way. This means fully entering into a new community and not holding back or walling off part of one's life from the new location. Incarnation is a full-time, full-life experience that demands the complete entering of a new way of being. In doing so, the missionary learns about the context and needs and concerns of the people whom she hopes to serve. Nor is true incarnational mission something that happens immediately or a task that can be reduced to a few weeks. It is a careful and lengthy process of learning and being that stretches on for years. It is worth remembering that Jesus lived on earth for 30 years before he began his ministry and that his entire life was devoted to one narrow and particular part of a vast world.

As Christ made himself vulnerable by living on earth, a central task for missionaries is to choose to give up the power and privilege inherent in their background and make themselves vulnerable to those with whom they work. This is especially true for missionaries from the developed world who head to the Global South and bring with them immense personal privilege, wealth, and education. Vulnerability is not a value that is highly prized in a Western culture that rewards dominance. Yet vulnerability is exactly what Christ chose to expose himself to and what missionaries must as well, with all the nerve-jangling, mind-warping, and uncomfortable effects that creates. Admittedly, it is likely impossible for missionaries fully to leave behind their backgrounds, nor is this always desirable because that background is often helpful in mission. But the lesson of the Incarnation is that missionaries must generally seek not the security of the inns but the vulnerability of the manger as they move into their new locations.

Once missionaries begin to learn from this shared existence and make themselves vulnerable, the information and messages they share will come to be shared in culturally-appropriate and -sensitive ways. This is at the core of mission communication. A message that can't be understood is no message at all. A message that is obeyed only because it comes from one who is more powerful will not last long. The history of mission is full of examples of times when a missionary's message was tragically, grievously, or comically misunderstood because the missionary failed to understand the context in which he was working. Incarnational mission works to avoid this pitfall by putting the emphasis on ensuring the missionary learns about the local context.

Seeing mission as truly incarnational has tremendous implications. First, it means that mission is not quantifiable in the way that the dominant culture of the western, developed world demands. Missionaries have long faced pressure to put their mission in terms of numbers. Francis Xavier, for instance, was forever reporting on the number of baptisms he had performed. Other missionaries have had to produce reports on the success of their schools or hospitals and how they were spending their money. But on the incarnational account, mission is not about the number of baptisms performed or students taught or sermons preached.

Mission is about existence, and existence is not something that is easily measurable. Missionaries simply are, in a new place.

A corollary to this idea is that mission is not about the results it produces but about the relationships it builds. The primary fruit of sharing an existence in a new place in a spirit of vulnerability is the connections and ties that are built between people of different backgrounds. Jesus spent a good deal of his ministry sharing meals—and building relationships—with people like the tax collectors who were outcast in society (e.g. Luke 19:1-10). This is again a challenging idea in the context of a Western, globalizing culture that prizes results that can be easily measured. But how are the quality and depth of relationships to be measured? Measurable results are not what are demanded by incarnational mission. Incarnational mission is, rather, about building relationships and those relationships cannot be quantified.

A second implication of this view of mission is that central to the mission imperative is that people must truly commit to people. In the Incarnation, God became human and committed to humans to the extent that Christ died for humans on the cross. This is what mission is all about—people loving, serving, and sacrificing for others in the name of restoring the right relationships that existed in Creation. Because of the relationships that are the fruit of incarnational mission, people learn about people as they really are and are more willing to make these sorts of commitments for one another. And there is a particular kind of people to commit to. God chose to cross the human-divine realm, a mammoth difference. In a similar way, if mission isn't engaging the multiple forms of difference in this world and crossing the barrier between secure and insecure, it's not mission. As Christ was sent to difference, so too are missionaries sent to commit themselves to those who, initially at least, appear most different.

Third, mission can happen anywhere and all the time. Christ's incarnational ministry was never "turned off." Because of the way in which he lived his life, opportunities for reconciliation continually presented themselves, so much so that he often had to step away from his busy life for a break (e.g. Matt. 14:13). Because the need for reconciliation is equally great around the world, missionaries can be both those who cross the ocean in search of difference and also those who find difference just down the street they've always known. Regardless of where the opportunity for incarnational ministry is found, the first question remains the same: How can I share an existence and be present with these people in a new way?

There remains a notable difference between Christ's Incarnation and our own efforts at incarnational mission: humans are sinful beings; Christ was not. The effects of human sin are multiple and profound and affect the very core of mission. It can make missionaries forget about the importance of vulnerability and start acting like their expertise is universally applicable. It can create suspicion and resentment when missionaries arrive and begin to share an existence in a new community. It can prevent people from truly listening to one another and learning about their different backgrounds and contexts, thereby impeding true relationship. Missionaries from the developed world to the Global South in particular enter mission with the baggage of a past that has often been sinful and exploitative of the people they seek to serve. Missionaries begin relationships in sin and continue to perpetuate it because of who they are.

Moreover, none of us is God in the way that Christ was. Few of us have the stamina or energy or perseverance that Christ did to carry on an exhausting ministry over the course of many years. The incarnational missiology in this paper needs to be tempered with a dose of realism. It is not, perhaps, practical to expect humans to continually be giving up power, crossing boundaries of difference, and building relationships. In that case, the principles laid out here are perhaps best seen as ideals toward which we must move in mission. The mission efforts of human beings will never achieve the perfect reconciliation embodied by Christ on the cross. But that is to be expected, given the reality of sin and our own failings. We still must move forward, aware of Christ's model and our own imperfections.

The incarnational missiology in this paper can be seen to be putting the emphasis squarely—perhaps too squarely—on the missionary. In discussing how a missionary can properly be in his or her new setting, this missiology can be criticized for barely mentioning the role-played the people among whom the missionary is to be. If God is truly to be at the centre of missiology and the *missio Dei* is to guide us, emphasizing the missionary's role seems doubly foolish. Yet it is precisely the *missio Dei* that is central on this account. God's loving action in the world—supremely expressed in the life, death, and resurrection of Jesus Christ—calls all of God's followers to restore right relationship in the world. As a result, all are missionaries and all are called to model their missional Christian service on the incarnational model set by Christ. Seeing mission in this incarnational light usefully expands the familiar definition of mission and makes it available and accessible to all Christians, wherever and however they may be.

While this paper affirms the centrality of the Incarnation to mission, it does not deny the importance of the cross. As Paul makes clear in Romans, Christ is a new Adam, whose obedience to the point of death atoned for the Adam's sin. It is through Christ's life and death that we are to "receive the abundance of grace and the free of gift of righteousness [to] exercise dominion in life". (Romans 5:17) We cannot forget, however, the ways in which the Incarnation laid the foundation for the later reconciling work of

Christ. Mission happens between the Incarnation and the cross in that the former lays the necessary foundation for the latter.

While there are many examples of humble, servant missionaries in Christian history, in general, this idea of incarnational mission does not appear to have held much purchase in historical mission. One common stereotyped view of past mission sees the missionary as a white male from the developed world who arrives in a community and begins preaching and baptizing with little regard for the cultural context and no interest in giving up any of the power he has inherent in his position. Another historical model of mission in which missionaries set up hospitals and schools is incarnational only insofar as those hospitals and schools are built and operated in consultation with the community and in response to their direct needs and desires. Yet history tells us that often this was not the case.

Mission and missiology has been seriously reconsidered in the last several decades to account for a world transformed by the end of colonialism, the emergence of a vibrant Christianity in the Global South, and improved global communication. One contemporary model for mission that has been a result of this rethink is the commitment by many mainline Protestant churches in the United States to the Millennium Development Goals (MDGs). These are the so-called "Eight Commandments" developed by the United Nations that arguably point the way to a more just future. Churches have been encouraged to donate a set percentage of their budget to MDG work around the world. The result has been that many congregations have gone scurrying to find organizations to which they can send money to fulfill the MDG budget line. In the run-up to the 2009 General Convention of the Episcopal Church, for example, major dissent arose when a budget committee removed a dedicated line for the MDGs with the reasonable justification that many other parts of the budget funded actual programs the were in line with the goals expressed by the MDGs. The first question for many churches seems to be not, "How can we share a new existence with people who are different to us?" or "How can we commit to people?" but "Where can we send the money?" While many churches are working to overcome this model of mission, it still holds sway in too many churches. Incarnational mission is different in that it puts the focus first on existence-sharing and relationship-building as the way to make sustainable progress towards reconciliation. If money enters the picture it is not as a first step.

Mission and missiology in the 21st-century is best served by returning to the model of Christ set in the Incarnation. This is a model that prizes the sharing of a common existence, the decision to give up power and make oneself vulnerable, and culturally-specific communications. This is what Christ modeled for us and what necessarily preceded his death and resurrection. If our efforts are properly incarnational, we will be laying the groundwork for rich and enriching mission, that sees people commit to people both in their local communities and around the world in service to the reconciling mission of God.

END NOTES

1. Jesse Zink was born in Canada and raised in the United States. He is a former missionary of the Episcopal Church in Mthatha, South Africa and recently completed his first year at Yale Divinity School in New Haven, Connecticut.

2. All Scripture quotations are from the New Revised Standard Version.

8

Living the Magnificat: The Blessed Virgin Mary as Model and Inspiration for Ecumenical Mission

Mission and Unity: Ecclesiology and Mission

Luiz Coelho[1]

Although several denominations have entered into ecumenical dialogue regarding the role of the Blessed Virgin Mary in the life of the Church, a universal Mariology is yet to be accepted among Christians of different confessions. While Christians in general are able to agree on the nature and works of Our Lord Jesus Christ, there still remains disagreement within ecumenical circles concerning what role the Blessed Virgin Mary plays in salvation history, and how she should, or should not, be venerated. As a result, ecumenical missiological dialogue has generally ignored the role of the Mother of Our Lord in the Church's ongoing mission in the world.

But the story we learn through Holy Scripture and Church Tradition grants great significance to her ministry with Christ. The Blessed Virgin Mary's witness is a source of hope and encouragement to Christians engaged in mission in a variety of contexts and eras. Christians from all traditions will always be able to learn a great deal about Jesus' path by following her footsteps. The Blessed Virgin Mary is, therefore, an inspiring example to all of us who carry on the task of fulfilling the mission of Christ's Church.

MARY: HUMBLE AND POOR

Although Holy Tradition has passed down beautiful stories about Mary's birth and childhood, we actually know very little historical information about the Virgin Mother's background. Scripture does tell us that she lived in the town of Nazareth, in Galilee (Lk 1:26). This region was, most likely, a multi-ethnic grouping of villages, which had been conquered by the Hasmoneans roughly a century before and resettled with Jews. It is safe to say, however, that her origins were not exactly noble. Galilee was far from the central power of Judea and its villages were poor in contrast to the luxury of larger cities. It was "part of an occupied state under the heel of imperial Rome. Revolution was in the air. The atmosphere was tense. Violence and poverty prevailed."[2]

Mary was, then, a representative of the large population of peasants, who made up the quasi-totality of the people in that region. It is noteworthy that she was betrothed to a man who was descended from the house of David, but the line of David itself contained ancestors who would not necessarily be classified as noble. In fact, Joseph, Mary's betrothed, was in the peasant class as well. In that regard, the Virgin's status as a poor woman is representative of many Christians, who have been called from the midst of the poor, to work with and for the poor and rich alike, in the name of God. Moreover, she stands as a role model of Christian poverty of spirit and a discipleship of utter trust and dependence on God.

By walking with Mary, we discover that God is always willing to surprise us and raise vocations in the most unpredictable places, especially among those who, despite their humble origins, are willing to obey the Almighty's will.

MARY: BELIEVER AND SERVANT

Perhaps one of the most striking moments of the Christian story is the Annunciation, the narrative of the Archangel Gabriel's visit to the Virgin Mary, through which she learns she has been chosen by God to conceive the Son of God in her womb (Lk 1:26-38). The story unfolds in a mix of tension, prophecy and joyful acceptance. In all, it is impressive to notice how Mary's attitude quickly changes from awe and concern to a full embrace of God's will.

Certainly, one cannot downplay her faith and courage that enabled her to accept such a mission. It is not every day that an angel appears announcing the miraculous birth of the Savior of the World. In a certain sense, her obedience relates directly to what Kierkegaard would call a "great leap of faith." "The purity of faith that Kierkegaard so admired in Abraham is here drawn to the apex of intensity."[3]

This is perhaps the main reason for praising Mary in the life of the Church. As Reformed Theologian Karl Barth put it, through Mary, humankind is revealed in the encounter: "the creature says 'Yes' to God….[E]very time people want to fly from this miracle," they "conjure away the mystery of the unity of God and man in Jesus Christ, the mystery of God's free grace."[4] In so many ways, Mary's faith is very similar to our own faith. She, the first believer, accepted Jesus Christ completely by faith, unlike the early disciples of Jesus needed signs and wonders to lead them to belief.

Christian Mission demands of us a leap of faith. The call to carry on Christ's work in the world is certainly daunting. It is often impossible according to human parameters. And yet, it beckons us to joyfully accept the work of Christ and to become engaged with it, because Mission ultimately points to God's work, and our response to that should be faithfully discerning how to foresee and act according to God's will, even if we cannot fully comprehend it. Mary said yes to God, even without fully knowing the implications of her obedience. Later, as the Incarnation unfolds and the poor of the world come to worship the Creator of the Universe dressed in the flesh of a poor peasant newborn infant, she herself treasures the experience in her heart (Lk 2:19), like the mystic Prophet Daniel (Dan 7:28) and other visionaries who reflect "on a mysterious revelation, only part of which he has fully understood."[5]

"The Annunciation scene, as biblically analyzed today, depicts her being called to the vocation of being God's partner in the work of redemption on the model of the call to Moses at the burning bush."[6] Like Mary, we are also called to be God's partners, reaching out to those in need. Following the leap of faith first taken by the Virgin of Nazareth, we too should declare in faith: "Here am I, the servant of the Lord; let it be with me according to your word" (Lk 1:38 NRSV).

MARY: FULL OF GRACE AND BLESSED

In the Annunciation narrative, the Angel refers to the Virgin Mary as "highly favored," and "full of grace." This suggests that she had a standard of holiness above other women, so that she was chosen by God to carry on God's will. In fact, as St. Ambrose of Milan would say, she was "so pure that she was chosen to be the Mother of the Lord. God made her whom He had chosen and chose her of whom He would be made."[7]

Intrinsically linked with Mary's acceptance of God's will in her life is the title bestowed upon her by God, and perpetuated by the Church over the Centuries: Blessed. As her cousin St.

Elizabeth pointed out, she is blessed among women (Lk 1:45), for she believed that which was impossible to believe.

Both expressions were soon merged by the Church in prayers, hymns of praise and antiphons, which would lead to formulas such as the Eastern Angelic Salutation and the Western Ave Maria, or Hail Mary. These venerable titles for the Blessed Virgin Mary are foundational to the Church's theological reflections, because they remind us of a constant need to strive for sanctification. Even though we cannot become God in essence, we can become "gods" by grace, as creatures of a human nature. This concept is better expressed by Eastern Christian Theology as Deification, or *Theosis*. "[T]he incarnation also presents the vocation of man-godhood as a new moral imperative, that men strive to imitate this Jesus Christ who is both archetype and perfect example of a deified humanity."[8] Especially in the encounter with the other, it is imperative that Christians be perceived as righteous, pure and holy: blessed and a blessing to those who surround them. The Virgin Mary was the first to be full of grace and deified. Her holiness points the way to Christ and to our own work in the world which both moves us towards *theosis*, while pointing the way for others to find Christ in and through our words and actions as representatives of Christ's body active in the world, like Mary, blessing the poor and liberating the oppressed.

MARY: PROPHET OF GOD'S JUSTICE

The Blessed Virgin Mary is often praised for her humbleness, calmness and resilience. Those qualities are certainly true to her character; however, one would be mistaken to think that those qualities make her unimportant. Blessed Mary is also a very important prophetic voice in the Church. She was poor, and lowly. She was a woman in a patriarchal society. She was a "nobody," but the Almighty chose to do wonderful things to her. Her song of praise, the Magnificat

(Lk 1:46-55), deeply expresses her gratitude and faithfulness to the Holy One's love for her. However, Mary's Song is more than a hymn of thanksgiving. It is a prophetic utterance through which Mary also announces God's justice to all the poor who fear Him. She proclaims a divine justice, which brings down the proud and mighty from their thrones, and exalts the lowly. She exclaims God's faithfulness to fill the hungry with good things, and warns the rich who trust in themselves that God will send them away empty. The Magnificat is a bold, revolutionary proclamation of God's justice for the poor and the meek, uttered by poorest of the poor who had been raised up by God, and filled with grace and blessing, so that she in turn could offer blessing to the world. Blessed Mary, empowered by the Holy Spirit, "embodies the nobodies of this world, on whom God is lavishing rescue.... This is a great prayer; it is a revolutionary song of salvation."[9]

Thus, Holy Mary is a witness of God's inclusive love. The poor Virgin from Nazareth, whose song of praise is the longest text attributed to a woman in the New Testament,[10] proclaims the coming of the Reign of God, and its social revolution that will redeem all people. Mary is, therefore, a partner in our hope that all of the oppressed will be ultimately liberated by the Mighty One. Christian Mission, likewise, must be as bold as the prophetic voice of the Blessed Virgin Mary. Otherwise, it becomes irrelevant in a world full of inequalities. If we conform to the corrupt and demonic power structures of this world, then we cannot proclaim, with Mary, the coming of God's Reign. Rather, we are called, like Mary, to be conformed to Christ, and to pray for the coming of God's Realm of justice and peace.

MARY: MOTHER

The fact that the Blessed Lady conceived Our Lord Jesus is not unknown to any Christian. Even most Christian children can name Mary as the mother of Jesus Christ. But, what does it mean to be a mother? What does it mean to be the mother of Jesus?

The physicality of the mother-child relationship begins from the moment of conception. St. Joseph certainly loved and cared for Jesus, even though he was not his biological father. But his wife experienced a relationship with Jesus that is unique to mothers. Her own body nurtured the embryonic Jesus as he grew in her womb. Her breasts fed him in his infancy, and her tender caresses and kisses embraced her infant son in maternal love and bliss. The First Council of Ephesus (431 AD) declared Blessed Mary to be not merely the mother of the human nature of Jesus, but called her *Theotokos*: God-bearer. When one thinks of the physical relationship that exists between a mother and a child, recognizing the child's utter dependence upon the mother for emotional and physical well being, alongside the mystery of Blessed Mary being the God-bearer, the Mother of God, one can not help but stand in awe in God's loving willingness to share the fragile nature of our humanity.

Early Christian iconography soon developed a pattern of representing the Virgin and her infant son in a tight embrace: an embrace of mutual love and care. Like many mothers, Mary was concerned about her son's care and protection. Jesus was raised during distressing times. His mother's concerns for him were not very different from the concerns of so many mothers today. Will this baby I carry in my arms survive childhood? Will he be healthy and free from diseases? Will we be able to feed him and clothe him? What if war, or violence, erupts in these lands? How will he be safe? How will I teach him the values that will enable him to grow to be an honest, compassionate, and holy person? Mary, like so many mothers, wanted her son to be healthy, happy, secure and safe; but, she soon learns that his path will take him to inevitable pain and suffering. As she is not able to do prevent the suffering that lies before her son, nor protect him from it, she accepts suffering with Him, and with his community, and learns to see her pain as a gateway to salvation, and as a conduit for God's presence with God's people.

How do we "bear God" in our own distressing times? One is reminded of the dialogue between Jesus and Nicodemus concerning "new birth", and as surely we know that bearing God for us happens in the same kind of mystical and spiritual experience that enacts our new birth in Christ. Bearing God, for us, includes allowing the Christ to be born within us, and within others, as we seek and serve Christ in the lives of those in need (Mt 23:35). A truly incarnational faith asks us to be like Blessed Mary, and to "give birth," to Christ among the ones we serve, seeing the very face of Christ in their faces, and in the faces of every human being, and doing whatever we can to care for them, to love them, to protect them and to serve them, as if they were Christ.

MARY: INTERCESSOR

At the Wedding in Cana (Jn 2:1-12), we learn of a Mary who intercedes to her Son on behalf of those in need. The reason might sound silly to some at a first glance: there was no more wine! At first Jesus is hesitant to act, as he explains to his mother that the time for him to be glorified has not yet come. However, in the end he performs the miracle, perhaps because of her persistent faith and trust in Jesus. Mary intercedes to him on behalf of those in need, already trusting he will do whatever is more appropriate to the situation. And in the end, she says: "Do whatever he tells you." (Jn 2:5 NRSV)

Mary's role as an intercessor in this story might be subtle, but it certainly teaches us to be bold in our asking and trusting of God above anything else. As we intercede for ourselves and for others, let us not be afraid to ask God to provide what we need, trusting that God's will is good for us, and will be done.

Any mission-oriented task must rely on a network of intercessors that connects those who are working in the mission field with those who support them remotely. Prayer is a powerful means of uniting the people of God in their needs, and through it we are able to share some of the pain that those who are engaged in the Mission of the Church feel. If we believe the Communion of Saints is connected through prayer, we must never forget to pray for our brothers and sisters in Christ and ask for their prayers too.

And let us not forget the Mother's final words: "Do whatever he tells you." Apart from being supported by prayer, Mission has to be Christ-Centered. This means that, at all times and in all places, we ought to keep in mind that whatever we do must be done according to our God's will. God in Christ left us several teachings that hint at what His will is. Christ-Centered Mission never stops to ask if its measures are compatible with the Mind of Christ, to which his mother gently points.

MARY: SUFFERER

How miserable the Mother of our Savior must have been as she contemplated her sinless son being sacrificed for our own salvation? The mother who suffers at the foot of the cross (Jn 19:25-27) has become a traditional theme in Christian Sacred Art. There, she joins St. John and other faithful women, who remained loyal to Jesus to the end. Despite their fear and pain, they knew it was time for Jesus to finish the work he had to do (Jn 19:28).

As Blessed Mary suffers with her son, Jesus has compassion upon her and makes her the mother of the Beloved Disciple, committing each to the mutual care of the other. By this gift, Jesus extends his family to all of his disciples. In Mark, when asked who his family is, Jesus clearly says that those who do God's will are his family (Mk 3:35). "If in Mark and Matthew there was a contrast between two families, one by nature and the other by discipleship, in John (as in Luke) the natural mother is brought into the family of discipleship in a preeminent way."[11]

Since in our Baptisms we have been born into this same family in Christ, we are called to share in the sufferings of each member of the family, as we gladly share in the rejoicings. Holy Mary and those who suffered near the cross consoled each other, prayed and worked together trusting it was not the end. Indeed it was not. Jesus would rise from the dead in three days, and all creation would be transformed. It was not the end: it was the beginning.

The call to Missions calls us to join Blessed Mary, John and all of Jesus' disciples in the task of bearing each other's pain and sorrow, if we truly are to be God's family. A missionary heart asks us to support and pray for those who suffer at the feet of the cross. In today's world, where calamities happen every single moment, this is even more imperative. Sharing the pain, building communities—families indeed: this is what we see in Blessed Mary's example, and this is what pleases our Lord.

MARY: GLORIFIED BY GOD, PRAISED BY THE CHURCH
No scriptural source describes how the Mother of God left this world. All we know from Scripture is that she was in a prominent position among those who received the Holy Spirit on Pentecost (Acts 1:13-14). Early Church Tradition, however, tells this story, which eventually evolved into a feast day, celebrated by most Eastern Christians, and some Western ones, as the Feast of the Dormition of the *Theotokos*, and by Roman Catholics as the Feast of the Assumption of the Blessed Virgin Mary, in which it is believed she was assumed body and soul into heaven. Many, but not all, Protestants chose not to speculate on her passing, and refrain from defining any doctrinal significance to her falling asleep, since they follow the Sola Scriptura principle.

However, it is safe to say that the Anglican collect for the Feast of the (Falling Asleep of) St. Mary the Virgin[12] expresses a statement that most Christians would be willing to agree on:

> O God, you have taken to thyself the blessed Virgin Mary, mother of thy incarnate Son: Grant that we, who have been redeemed by his blood, may share with her the glory of thine eternal kingdom; through the same thy Son Jesus Christ our Lord, who liveth and reigneth with thee, in the unity of the Holy Spirit, one God, now and for ever. Amen.[13]

There is no doubt that the Mother of God, a lady of impressive faith and virtue, was embraced by God at the moment of her death. It was an embrace of love. And this same Lady continues to be praised and remembered by the Church, in readings, prayers, hymns and antiphons. With her, multitudes of saints and heavenly creatures ceaselessly praise our Lord and God.

May we learn, as we do the Mission of the Church, how to pursue this path of sainthood, and follow the steps of the Blessed Lady in imitating Christ. May we learn to be faithful believers even in the midst of grief and sorrow. May we learn how to be prophets, and ceaselessly proclaim God's justice and liberation. May we in all things allow God to speak and act through us. Those are basic principles for Mission that can be applied irrespective of where, when or how we are serving. And in our faithfulness, God will embrace us with an irresistible embrace of love that reaches out to the whole world.

END NOTES

1. Luiz Coelho is an Engineer, Visual Artist, and Ordained from the Anglican Diocese of Rio de Janeiro, Brazil. His multidisciplinary work focuses mostly on the intersections between Sacred Art, Liturgy, Mission and Technology.

2. Elizabeth Johnson, "In Search of the Real Mary," *Catholic Update* (May 2001).

3. W. Paul Jones. "Mariology: An Unrecognized Entree to Ecumenical Dialogue," *The Journal of Religion* 44, no. 3 (1964), http://jstor.org/stable/1200813 (accessed December 15, 2009), 217.

4. Ibid, 219

5. Raymond Brown, "Mary: The First Disciple," *Scripture from Scratch* (May 1997).

6. Elizabeth Johnson, "In Search of the Real Mary," *Catholic Update* (May 2001).

7. John A. Hammes, "The Patristic Praise of Mary," *Faith and Reason* (Summer 1990).

8. Vigen Guroian. "Notes Toward an Eastern Orthodox Ethic," *The Journal of Religious Ethics* 9, no. 2 (1981), http://jstor. org/stable/40014936 (accessed December 15, 2009), 231.

9. Elizabeth Johnson, "In Search of the Real Mary," *Catholic Update* (May 2001).

10. Ibid.

11. Raymond Brown, "Mary: The First Disciple," *Scripture from Scratch* (May 1997).

12. While most Books of Common Prayer call this feast only "St. Mary the Virgin," some books, most notably the Scottish and Canadian ones, have restored the full name "the Falling Asleep of St. Mary the Virgin."

13. *The Book of Common Prayer*, 192.

BIBLIOGRAPHY

Brown, Raymond. "Mary: The First Disciple," *Scripture from Scratch*, May 1997.

Elizondo, Virgilio. *Guadalupe: Mother of the New Creation.* Markinoll, NY: Orbis Books, 1997.

Gambrero, Luigi. *Mary and the Fathers of the Church: The Blessed Virgin Mary in Patristic Thought.* San Francisco: Ignatius Press, 1999.

Guroian, Vigen. "Notes Toward an Eastern Orthodox Ethic," *The Journal of Religious Ethics* 9, no. 2 (1981): 228-244. http://www.jstor.org/stable/40014936 (accessed December 15, 2009).

Hammes, John A. "The Patristic Praise of Mary," *Faith and Reason*, Summer 1990.

Pangborn, Cyrus R. "Christian Theology and the Dogma of the Assumption," *Journal of Bible and Religion* 30, no. 2 (1962): 93-100. http://www.jstor.org/stable/1459737 (accessed December 15, 2009).

Jones, W. Paul. "Mariology: An Unrecognized Entree to Ecumenical Dialogue," *The Journal of Religion* 44, no. 3 (1964): 210-222. http://www.jstor.org/stable/1200813 (accessed December 15, 2009).

Johnson, Elizabeth. "In Search of the Real Mary," *Catholic Update*, May 2001.

Pelikan, Jaroslav. *Mary Through the Centuries.* Yale University Press, 1998.

The Book of Common Prayer. Church Publishing, 1979.

9

Reclaiming the Church's Mission in the Light of Missio Dei

Foundations for Mission

John Hyunjoon Park[1]

J ust before Jesus ascended to heaven, His disciples and followers were eager and convinced that the *Parousia*, which the Scripture had long promised, was near. Disappointingly, Jesus claimed that it was not for them to know the time and date, as this authority rests with the Father. The letters in the New Testament seem to suggest that the disciples and followers of Jesus believed the *Parousia* would be soon.

Interestingly, this belief in the imminence of the *Parousia* has survived in and out of Christian communities over two millennia. The Scripture certainly suggests that Christians must always be wakeful because the day of the Lord will come like a thief in the night.[2] However, one must ask oneself if her/his reaction to this immanence resembles the reaction that the disciples and followers had: "They were looking intently up into the sky as he was going, when suddenly two men dressed in white stood beside them. 'Men of Galilee,' they said, 'why do you stand here looking into the sky?'"[3]

Christian hope in any capacity should not be simplistic and superficial optimism that Fensham describes in terms of the dystopic metaphor of a "Dark Age Ahead."[4] At the time of the 1910 Edinburgh World Missionary Conference, there seemed to be an underlying expectation about the possibility of evangelizing the entire world in that generation.[5] It is evident that the Church had benefited from being dominant at least within the Western world. Bosch argues, "Reading theological treatises from earlier centuries, one gets the impression that there was only church, no world. Put differently, the church was a world on its own. Outside the church there was only the 'false church.'"[6] However, contrary to its expectations, the Church has lost its position in relationship to the world. The Church seems to be wondering if it is due to the rapid changes within the world, or even if there is a flaw in Christian belief. Being relevant and using the most up-to-date technology become top-priority and favoured, the Church seems to be abandoning the rich traditions and poetry of Christianity.

This paper argues that the mission of the Church can truly be life-giving when it is constructed in the light of the mission of God, *Missio Dei*, and in that light, the Church is called to live and bring the reign of God amid daily life. Both Church and mission find their true meaning in God's salvific work, which should be an overarching concept for them.[7] God has been eagerly reaching God's arm of loving covenant out to the world since the time of creation, and in whichever generation and world the Church is situated, it is to carry the same compassionate heart to the ends of the earth.

MISSIO DEI

Theological reflection on the Church's mission in the light of the *Missio Dei* should bring the reign of God to the center of the Church rather than making the Church its focus. The reign of God should be the norm that everything must be measured against. What God is up to is what the Church should be up to. Practically speaking, a church's mission statement is not where the church's interests and wishes are filled, but where the *Missio Dei* is discerned in the practices and work of the church.

This task of bringing the reign of God into reality can only be possible when the Church is willing to understand the world, itself, mission, the Scriptures, God and everything from God's perspective. One can begin to see a glimpse of the Divine plan by letting go of one's own selfish concerns. The Scripture states, "Since, then, you have been raised with Christ, set your hearts on things above, where Christ is seated at the right hand of God. Set your mind on things above, not on earthly things. For you died, and your life is now hidden with Christ in God."[8] The author of the letter to the Colossians instructs readers to set their minds on the reign of Christ, things above and beyond the interests of merely human standards. Often the Church does not operate out of such profound standards of love and community but rather mundane and self-indulgent standards. The Scriptures are very clear about the death of self-interest and self-exaltation.

Through the reconstruction of the Church's mission in the light of *Missio Dei*, the Church should seek to see the reign of God amid the lives of individuals, communities and their interactions. There is an irresistible calling for each individual and community to be perfect as the Father is;[9] this calling can only be possible when one is completely owned by the Father through the empowerment of the Holy Spirit in Christ. The wholeness of God is expanded by God-self to bring the fullness of life into every corner of the world where God's grace extends.

Some often tend to interpret this wholeness only in its spiritual aspect while others materialize everything. Wholeness is about bringing fullness into every aspect of life: material, spiritual and mental. The Christian community in Thessalonica was given a blessing in the letter to them, "May your whole spirit, soul and body be kept blameless at the coming of our Lord Jesus Christ."[10] Whether or not this blessing was influenced by the belief in the immanence of *Parousia* at the period, it is evident that as Christians there is a hope and expectation of the wholeness in every aspect of life.

The source of Christian hope lies in God's promise. The Hebrew Scripture had constantly witnessed to God's faithfulness to promises through God's delivery and restoration. The author of Philippians picks up this theme and argues with confidence that "he who began a good work in you will carry it on to completion until the day of Christ Jesus."[11] The hope of Christianity blossoms from the foundation of God's promises with God's people; both the covenants in the Old and New Testaments are partly and essentially God's faithful promises to nurture them and to deliver them from all evil in the fullness of time. What is required from God's people is to support God's vision by trusting in the Lord and acting with the hope based on God's promises.

The reign of God can be discerned from our limited human perspective by reconsidering what God is up to in God's grand plan. It is God's plan, not the Church's, and it is God who reigns, not the Church; thus it is important for the Church to constantly reassess itself and often with the aid of outside criticism. Does the Church's mission truly envision the reign of God? Do benefits go only to the Church or to all? Does God have ownership of the Church and its mission or the Church? Just as God had constantly sent prophets to the Israelites to re-examine their lives and responsibilities, God has given the Church the Scripture and the Holy Spirit to re-evaluate its life and responsibilities and to call us into action.

The Church's mission

By handing over the ownership of the Church and mission to God, the Church can become God's sign and symbol. When the Church's mission is stalled over the issue of ownership, mission can easily turn into nothing more than a means for the Church to instigate what is of its own self-interest and restore the *Corpus Christianum*.[12] The true calling for the Church is, however, to follow Christ's example, risking and losing its own life for the sake of others, and most importantly, to proclaim that God has prepared a new way for the world to live through the life, death and resurrection of the Lord Jesus Christ. The fullness of life is found in Christ, not in the Church; the Church is to resemble Christ, whose Spirit is the source of life, not to become the source itself to the world.

Reflecting on the role and function of the Church in the world in regards to the reign of God, one can picture the Church with respect to the relationship between the maternal God and Her child. Bryan Jeong Guk Lee describes Jürgen Moltmann's concept of *ZimZum* as the relationship between mother and baby in her womb.[13] The feminine imagery of conception and birthing are observed in the Scripture and often picked up by some theologians; however, the use of this imagery was often limited only to describing God's maternal love. When the Church is depicted in regard to her relationship with God, the prominent picture is that the Father, who sent His Son, together with the Spirit, to sends the Church into the world.[14] While this is a valid and significant image of the Church, the maternal image of God captures what it overlooks. Appreciating the Church in the light of the maternal God reveals new meanings and insights that may help us to broaden our understanding of the Church.

In feminine imagery, the Church can be represented by the umbilical cord in the Mother's womb. In explaining the feminine imagery of God conceiving and giving birth, Lee explains, "she enters into the space *within* her ... for the benefit of the baby and reaches out with the umbilical cord through the space within *to* the baby to give it life."[15] In this female-biological picture, it is clear that the role of the Church is to transport the nourishment from the Mother to the baby. The whole purpose of the Church's existence is to become a channel between God and the world to come, and this is what the Church should and must strive to be. Bosch rightly claims, "To participate in mission is to participate in the movement of God's love toward people, since God is a fountain of sending love."[16] As much as the Church receives life and love from God, the Church is called to give them to the world, remembering that none of them are ever theirs.

According to the New Testament, the Church seems to be presented as the first sign—not the final destination—that God has chosen to fulfill God's grand redemptive plan. The Apostle Paul mentions in his letter to the Christians in Rome how the creation eagerly awaits and groans in the pains of childbirth for the completion of God's redemptive work.[17] There is a constant and underlying expectation since the time of creation that the baby, as the world, will grow and mature to her/his fullness, the point of being birthed. The Church as the umbilical cord is responsible to transport essential nourishments for the completion of the formation of the baby.

The labour pains in the Mother's womb signal the nearness of final delivery. This final delivery is comparable to the Scripture's description of the new heaven and earth; there is the expectation that what is never actualized in this world will come to reality in future. The Church is eschatological, meaning that "the Church is linked to the historical future, in realities that it faces daily, and the ultimate future, which is the purpose and meaning of God's creation."[18] We, as the Church, are part of and are involved in

God's redemptive work, which will result in a radical newness for the Church and the world in the ultimate future.

This newness in the future[19] is important for the Church to notice for several reasons. First, the Church is involved in more than just individual salvation; there is a greater vision at the creation of new heaven and earth. Bosch rightly claims,

> The church's missionary involvement suggests more than calling individuals into the church as a waiting room for the hereafter. Those to be evangelized are, with other human beings, subject to social, economic, and political conditions in this world. There is, therefore, a "convergence" between liberating individuals and peoples in history and proclaiming the final coming of God's reign.[20]

The Church should and must have the eyes that can see this vision that goes "beyond the poetry we taught our children."[21]

Second, the Church must constantly remind itself that the Church "has no fixed abode here; it is a paroikia, a temporary residence. It is permanently underway, toward the ends of the world and the end of time."[22] The true calling for the Church is to offer all the authority and power that was bestowed by the Lord to the others and ultimately to the Other, who is the Ultimate Ruler of all.

Lastly, the final delivery of the baby indicates that there will be a new relationship between God and the world.[23] In the womb, the baby might not fully acknowledge the existence and identity of the Mother; however, once s/he is born, the relationship is now re-established so that "we shall see face to face."[24] The Church thus must discern what its calling is in the midst of this new relationship. More importantly, the Church leaders are called to reflect theologically on the grand history of Christianity from the past to the present and future in God's promise, and address the Church where it should be led.

THE CHURCH TODAY

Taking into consideration that the grand-narrative of *Missio Dei* progresses towards the *Parousia*, the eagerly awaited birth of new heaven and earth, the Church in the present is called to partake in bearing the pains of labour. The cross calls the church to humility, even to the point of suffering and death for the sake of others. In the world that favours an increasing consumer self-gratification and dominance of exploitative structures, we Christians face a profound challenge to live lives that are willing to be relinquished in order for others to gain.

The reign of God brings fullness in every aspect of life, and the Church's mission should thus embrace all elements of what is considered life, and help lead others into the source of life, which is Christ. The aim of sharing the Good News should be what Israel expected the Messiah to do, to establish God's *shalom*, which brings a new life in the new aeon.[25] Jesus spoke on the issues of material well-being, healed the sick, took care of the poor, defended the defenceless, preached the Good News of the heavenly kingdom and suffered, entered and defeated death.

However, one must bear in mind that what is essential in the midst of all things is what is eternal. There will be a new heaven and earth, and the Church is called to work towards and in expectation of this ultimate future. Thus, embracing all elements of life is not becoming hindered by any aspect of life, but rather utilizing all elements to help us to ultimately grasp what is eternal and vital, that is the new, joyous and everlasting relationship in perfect harmony with the Triune God. The Scripture testifies that "All this is from God, who reconciled us to himself through Christ, and has given us the ministry of reconciliation; that is, in Christ God was reconciling the world to himself, not counting their trespasses against them, and entrusting the message of reconciliation to us."[26] The Good News re-establishes one's relationship with God, breaking down the walls of hardened heart towards the Lord and Saviour and also towards others.

Breaking down some of the walls and boundaries that the Church has maintained may often bring difficult challenges to us, especially in understanding the Church's relationship with the world; however, one must admit that the Church is a human institution. It is made up of fallible humans, and acknowledging this mortal characteristic of the Church is the first step for the Church to walk humbly with God in mission. This acknowledgement not only frees the Church from a fear of relinquishing its ownership—that there is a better Ruler to make things right—but also guides Christians to gratitude that the Sovereign God is willing to use imperfect beings to bring a fullness into the world; it is a great wonder that humbles the Church and submerges it into the *Missio Dei*.

Aligning the Church's mission with the *Missio Dei* is a humble and holy pilgrimage that requires the Church's complete trust in the Lord. The Church has received an irresistible invitation from the Lord to surrender its life and trust in God, making every opportunity to share the message of reconciliation and to do what is good in the eyes of the Lord.

Conclusion

Christians can easily lose their patience and confidence, as the world is rapidly changes. We should resist simplistic optimism and return to the heart of Christianity which is fed by the *Missio Dei*, otherwise mission is in danger of being reduced to methodology and strategy. The Church has been called to partake in the birth of the new heaven and earth, where the new and everlasting relationship with God rests. The Church and its mission belong to God, and God's grand-narrative redemptive plan is accomplished "not by might nor by power, but by [God's] Spirit [, says the Lord Almighty]."[27]

END NOTES

1. John Park is from Canada and a second year a master's degree student in M. Div. program at Knox College. He is currently the president of the Mission and Theological Society, the student association at Knox College. He also serves in Oakridge Presbyterian Church, London, Ontario, as a student minister.

2. 1 Thessalonians 5:2.

3. Acts 1:10-11.

4. The title of a book by C. Fensham. cf. The introductory chapter of the book.

5. Bosch, David J., *Transforming Mission: Paradigm Shifts in Theology of Mission* (Maryknoll, NY: Orbis Books, 1991), 337.

6. Bosch, *Transforming Mission*, 376.

7. Ibid., 370.

8. Colossians 3:1-3.

9. Matthew 5:48. In its commentary on Matthew, David Hill writes, "The emphasis is not on flawless moral character, but on whole-hearted devotion to the imitation of God—not in the perfection of his being, but of his ways. cf. Hill, David, *The Gospel of Matthew* (London: Oliphants, 1972), 131.

10. 1 Thessalonians 5:23.

11. Philippians 1:6. cf. Fowl, Stephen E., *Philippians* (Grand Rapids, MI: William B. Eerdsmans Publishing Company, 2005), 26-27.

12. Hoekendijk, J.C., *The Church Inside Out* (Philadelphia, PA: The Westminster Press, 1964), 15. Also cf. Hall, Douglas John, *The End of Christendom and the Future of Christianity* (Valley Forge, PA: Trinity Press International, 1997).

13. Lee uses the definition of ZinZum as "concentration and contraction, and signifies a withdrawing of oneself into oneself" from Moltmann, Jürgen, *God in Creation: A New Theology of Creation and the Spirit of God* (Minneapolis: Fortress Press, 1985), 87.

14. Bosch, *Transforming Mission*, 390.

15. Lee, Bryan Jeong Guk, *Celebrating God's Cosmic Perichoresis: The Eschatological Panentheism of Jürgen Moltmann as a Resource for an Ecological Christian Worship* [Italic Perochoresis] (Toronto, 2009), 73.

16. Bosch, *Transforming Mission*, 390. Understand God as a fountain of sending love is also John Calvin's core understanding in his Eucharistic theology. cf. Gerrish, Brian, "The Holy Banquet and the Sum of Piety," *Grace and Gratitude* (Minneapolis: Fortress Press, 1993).

17. Cf. Romans 8:19-22.

18. Fensham, Charles, *Emerging from the Dark Age Ahead: The Future of the North American Church* (Ottawa: Novalis Publishing, Inc., 2008), 13.

19. Moltmann discusses in detail about the term "Newness." cf. Moltmann, Jürgen, "The Category Novum," *The Coming of God* (London: SCM Press, 1996), 27-29.

20. Bosch, *Transforming Mission*, 377.

21. Fensham, *Emerging from the Dark Age Ahead*, 10.

22. Bosch, *Transforming Mission*, 374. The concept of viewing the church as a temporary residence is also evident in *Dogmatic Constitution on the Church: Lumen gentium* (Boston: St. Paul Editions, 1965).

23. In this paragraph, depending on theological norm, the world might be limited to humanity, as there seems to be no indication in the Scripture that the creation other than human beings does not acknowledge its Creator. In fact, Romans 8:20 indicates that the creation is subject to God, and many Psalms proclaim creation as worshipping God; for instance, "Let the fields be jubilant, and everything in them. Then all the trees of the forest will sing for joy." (Psalm 96:12)

24. 1 Corinthians 13:12.

25. Hoekendijk, The Church Inside Out, 21.

26. 2 Corinthians 5:18-19.

27. Zechariah 4:6

Bibliography

Bosch, David J. *Transforming Mission: Paradigm Shifts in Theology of Mission*. Maryknoll, NY: Orbis Books, 2002.

Fensham, Charles. *Emerging from the Dark Age Ahead: The Future of the North American Church*. Ottawa: Novalis, 2008.

Fowl, Stephen E. *Philippians*. Grand Rapids, MI: William B. Eerdsmans Publishing Company, 2005.

Gerrish, Brian, *Grace and Gratitude*. Minneapolis: Fortress Press, 1993.

Hall, Douglas John, *The End of Christendom and the Future of Christianity*. Valley Forge, PA: Trinity Press International, 1997.

Hill, David, *The Gospel of Matthew*. London: Oliphants, 1972.

Hoekendijk, J. C. *The Church Inside Out*. Philadelphia, PA: The Westminster Press, 1966.

Lee, Bryan Jeong Guk. *Celebrating God's Cosmic Perichoresis: The Eschatological Panentheism of Jürgen Moltmann as a Resource for an Ecological Christian Worship* [Italic Perochoresis]. Toronto, 2009.

Moltmann, Jürgen, *The Coming of God*. London: SCM Press, 1996.

10

Ligitation and Missions: How Do We Reach This Eclectic World?

Mission and Postmodernities

Patrick Stefan[1]

STANDING IN A NEW LAND

C hristianity today waves her banner in a world captured by an environment of change. Change is occurring on a grand scale in politics, technology, religion, and community. However, ultimately under-girding this environment is a foundational change of philosophy; the movement from modernism to post-modernism. The world has taken witness, modernity's scientific plight toward utopia has failed and so mankind has been left to crouch back into its cultural caves. Reality is now found within the assembly.

However, if culture determines reality, doesn't this by nature run contrary to the Scriptural testimony that there is no way to the Father but through the Son (John 14:6)? Western culture has completed its attempt at the industrialization of the world. We no longer strive to push toward one global culture; rather, we seek a fragmented world that paradoxically works together through the information age to create unity while maintaining cultural diversity. The church can no longer afford to ostracize itself from this reality. We must view our world mission as one that accounts for the postmodern world with both its positive and negative aspects.

THE PROSECUTION OF MODERNISM

Modernity, characterized by the enlightenment and its scientific plight, brought with it dreams of utopia. The removal of cultural boundaries to bring about conformity to the scientific way was thought to be the means by which we would solve the problems of hunger, crime, and war. Modernity desired to strip from our knowledge the myth or narrative of our world and transcend the story to reach the bare naked facts. Only then would we be able to bring about this modern utopia.

History though failed to bear out this scientific prophecy. As technology grew, countries began to expand, seeing their individual culture as *the* objective standard. With this came imperialistic conquest through colonization. Strong Western countries entered their colonies seeking to radically transform the receiving country from a narrative based understanding of the world to a "facts-based" scientific culture. However, what was born was not the utopia of enlightenment thought, but rather the reality of apartheid, mustard gas, slave trade, concentration camps with showers as death chambers, and ultimately the nuclear bomb.

Suspicions were raised in the minds of the people as a result of the false prophecies of modernism. Unfortunately, Christianity (specifically mission theory) was tied heavily to the prophet of modernism. Rather than injecting the gospel of Jesus Christ into the targeted culture, Christian missionaries sought generally to change the culture to pattern off Western ideals in order to present the gospel. Naturally then, as modernity stood on the witness stand for prosecution, people saw the church standing beside her.

Following the deliberation, what arose was a fragmented world in which every culture was now seen to create its own reality. The Western world lost its grasp on being the objective standard for knowledge. With this loss entered a new process of thought... Post-modernism. The question we must invite as a church is how we are to approach this new philosophy. The church's marriage to modernity brought scorn from society during the trial; will we make the same mistake with this new temptress?

The central argument of this paper is that the Christian mission theory must stand between modernity and post-modernity. In our theory of missions we must recognize both the positive and negative aspects of each philosophical view to devise a way in which we do not fall with post-modernism as we did with modernism. We must use the post-modern consciousness to the advantage of the church. Its critical assessment of the enlightenment can aid in our divorce from modernism. However, we must be critical thinkers so as to not travel down all provided roads.

The dismemberment of modernism as it concerns Christianity came from two primary angles: the philosophical question of knowledge and the cultural question of truth. Thus we enter into the courtroom to view the philosophical and cultural outcome of post-modernity and how our theory of missions should be shaped by it.

PHILOSOPHICAL CONSIDERATIONS

The introduction of post-modernism brought with it a shift in emphasis from the individual to the community. But why was this so? The foundational philosophical premise of the enlightenment was that mankind must crawl beneath the myth in order to attain the bare facts, viewing the world objectively. By doing this, we can harness the scientific method and achieve our utopian goal. It was, they said, the constraint of our presuppositions that keeps us from achieving this.

It was this foundational question that was challenged by the post-modern philosophers. Can we in fact leave behind our cultural conditions, our presuppositions, in order to view the world objectively? Further, is objective knowledge even possible? As knowledge and experience grew the many perspectives of the world became apparent. With this realization came the manifestation of another mounting problem, the recognition of the great chasm between sense perception and true reality.

Modernism asked the question of where the beginning of knowledge was found, and its answer was achieved by peering inside man himself. Modernism's epistemology placed man at the center of the universe. Just as the sun is the controlling entity in our solar system, governing all planets within its sphere, the mind of man was to modernism the center of the solar system of knowledge. But if the postmodern challenge is right, autonomous man is removed from the center of this system, thus creating a void that ultimately must be replaced by another controlling entity.

Post-modernism, realizing the inability of autonomous man, replaced him with the community within which each person resides. Thus, reality was now found in the assembly. It is now the community that creates the narrative, or story by which the adherents interpret the world. This story acts as the lens by which all gathered information filters through to produce meaning.

THE CHRISTIAN DILEMMA

The question that now approaches the Christian head on is how we present a gospel to a philosophical culture that proclaims "incredulity toward metanarratives"?[2] The Christian's immediate response is the observation that Christianity claims to be exactly that, one narrative that overarches all others. We must though ask the question if this is precisely what the post-modern mind means when they question the use of metanarratives.

Remember from where we have come thus far. Post-modernism has directly challenged modernism, not as a claim of an over-arching story but rather as a claim of objectivity in knowledge. It is this objectivity that is challenged by the post-modern. They recognize that objectivity in knowledge simply cannot be attained because of that little problem called 'interpretation.' Even if we pretend to gather the facts objectively we must still interpret them in light of our cultural condition. In recognition of this, they simply resort to the admission of the necessity of a story by which they can interpret the collected facts. For this reason they take refuge in their community which provides for them this story.

But isn't this also the testimony of Christianity? John Calvin saw the necessity of a narrative structured view of the world: "just as eyes, when dimmed with age or weakness or by some other defect, unless aided by spectacles, discern nothing distinctly; so, such is our feebleness, unless Scripture guides us in seeking God, we are immediately confused."[3] Without the revelation of God we are the blind, leading the blind (Matt 15:14). What is unique about Christianity is that it properly balances the dichotomy of individualism and community through the revelation of God. Man needs the revelation of God to properly see the world. This is his lens, and this lens ultimately breeds forth a community, the church, by which we see the world and interpret it according to God's revealed word.

Christian missionary activity can thrive in the post-modern world because it too accounts for the fallibility of man. The Christian world-view recognizes the inability of man set upon his lone island to process the information of the world. We must learn to harness these similarities to produce a mission that accounts for the realities of the post-modern recognition, while affirming the supremacy of Jesus Christ. Let us first reflect on the cultural considerations before we seek an answer to this dilemma.

Our philosophical considerations come to a head summarily in this point: post-modernism has rightly acknowledged the fallibility of man thus requiring a lens by which one can interpret the world. Our culture therefore becomes necessary; however, over and above this culture Christianity proclaims Scripture as the inspired interpretation of the world. We must explore further to see how these two categories can mold together.

CULTURAL CONSIDERATIONS

The philosophical discoveries of post-modernism led to an emphasis on cultural influence. The postmodern community finds refuge from her inability by clinging to the cultural construction. Each individual culture creates its own reality; it contains its own laws and religion. This explains the many interpretations of reality seen around the globe.

Interestingly though, in the modern information era we bring these cultures together to create a new utopia, a new hope for world peace. Rather than finding utopia in one culture championed throughout the world based upon the scientific plight, post-modernism seeks to eclectically join together the many cultures of the world into one unity. This is similar to the puzzle that is one large picture from afar, yet as the viewer creeps closer, she sees that each piece is its own individual picture making up the whole. Each piece represents each culture that works together to make one united picture.

This post-modern picture of the world shows us that Christianity's missionary endeavors can too often flock back to modernity, seeing our culture as superior to the ones into which we enter. Wilbert Shenk outlines three facts that have weakened missionary work: "the association of missions with aggressive imperialism…[the] attitude of European/Christian superiority toward other cultures and peoples; and… the divisions among Christians."[4] These traits all linger back to our relationship with modernism. The post-modern emphasis on culture has opened our eyes to our individual inability and allowed us to see ourselves in the appropriate light. Only when we see ourselves properly, as sinners in desperate need of the loving, redeeming grace of God through Jesus Christ can we then see other cultures and societies in their proper place, as sinners in desperate need of the loving, redeeming grace of God through Jesus Christ.

THE CALL OF RELATIVITY

This post-modern observation of cultural necessity brings with it a very important question for the Christian; is truth then relative to the culture? And if it is how can we claim superiority for Christianity and engage in missions? Relativity poses a large challenge to Christian missions because it raises the culture to a supreme level, and a necessary part of that culture is its religion. We must ask the question before engaging in Christian missions; does the religion we bring well up from within our culture, or do we see it as residing above our culture? Ultimately then, the Christian missionary is driven to the question of the interpretation of the world, are we carrying with us the banner of Western ideals, or the banner of Christ?

The Christian missionary now enters a new society as a cultural equal. He stands as an ambassador, but one not of Western traditions, one of Christ and His kingdom. The church must detach the gospel and the Holy Scriptures from Western civilization. The beauty of God's Word is that, unlike the Quran, it can be translated into any language. We cannot stop here though; we must also see that the

Bible can be translated into any way of thinking. Western culture thinks chronologically, historically which is largely different from other cultures. If we insist that the Christian religion is dependent on Western convention and thinking we immediately make it simply one of the many pieces that contribute to the large, eclectic puzzle. This is precisely what we cannot do because when we reach this point, we are merely proclaiming the supremacy of one piece of the puzzle over another.

We must change our view of the world as missionaries. To combat the call of relativity, we must place Scripture on a level above natural revelation. The first step toward this is to recognize our fallibility. View the thought patterns of the culture we enter as equal to us and from there seek to bring the gospel in through the road of contextualization.

CONTEXTUALIZING WITHOUT RELATIVIZING

Christian mission theory must be based upon the supremacy of Christ over all aspects of life. Notice carefully that in this statement there is no mention of the supremacy of any culture. Christ is not tied to one particular culture. This does not mean that we discard the fruits of Western growth. The great creeds and confessions that have grown from Western thought is what we build upon to provide our understanding of Holy writ. It is this understanding that we must then translate to the receiving nation.

In a very real sense, post-modernism is correct, we must see ourselves within our cultural environment. Only then can we recognize our presuppositions in order to see the world Scripturally. This is vital for the Christian to grasp before we can properly engage in missions. We bring Scripture into the culture and allow it (rather than Western ideals) to translate to the people. In other words, Scripture will seep into the minds and hearts of the readers and change the way they see the world.

Our message is the Bible, our understanding is the presuppositions of the historic, orthodox creeds, and the means should be those of the people we enter. The missionary should not enter ignorantly; he should come to the people thinking like them, seeking to bring the gospel to them to allow the Holy Spirit to transform the people. The focus should be on forming indigenous churches that are built by and on the people themselves. This foundation will remove Western traditions from the mind of the receptor. The truth of Scripture is our contention, not the truth of Europe or North America.

SCRIPTURAL CONSIDERATIONS

This message of contextualization is precisely the message of the Apostle Paul in 1 Corinthians 9:19-23. Paul adamantly proclaims that he will gladly leave behind his cultural upbringings so that the gospel might penetrate the hearts of all men. Further, he does not ask these people to change their culture. Paul continues to observe Jewish feasts (Acts 20:6). He even had his travelling partner, Timothy (an adult mind you), circumcised to reach the Jewish audience (Acts 16:1-4). Paul saw the gospel as so vitally important that its ambassadors must be willing to sacrifice who they are in order to be a part of the Kingdom of God and transmit His message.

In Matthew 28:18-20 we typically emphasize Jesus' words to 'go' into the world. However, when we look deeper, we find a different emphasis in this passage. Christ is telling his disciples not merely to go, but to go to the nations. We are to go to groups of people. Is Christ recognizing the necessity of national identity, the necessity for cultural context in knowledge? When we go to the nations we don't call them to be a new Western culture within their nation; rather, we baptize them in the name of the Triune God. We call them into the Kingdom of God through the gospel, which is contained in the Holy Scriptures transcending culture, thus allowing its translatability to the various people groups.

CONCLUSION: THE ECLECTIC UNITY

Post-modernism has prosecuted modernity and now stands as the zeitgeist, the philosophy of the day. In a large way, post-modernism has informed the Church of many important truths. It has reminded us of the importance of community, something Christianity has always proclaimed (Matt. 16:13-20). It has reminded us of the fallibility of man, something Christianity rests upon (Rom. 3:9-20). But perhaps most importantly, it has called us back to the necessity of a narrative by which we must interpret the world; it has reminded us of the importance of presuppositions.

For the Christian missionary, this reality opens a door by which Scripture can enter. It is no coincidence that God chose to give His revelation to us in the form of a story, a narrative. I propose that the central focus in missionary endeavors should be the history of redemption, from the first Adam to the second Adam (Rom. 5:12-21). This becomes the inspired narrative.

Scripture always calls us out of our nationalistic thinking to the knowledge of Christ as He is found in His Word. Yet in this we do not leave our culture. Scripture becomes the over-arching lens by which we view the world. It provides a grid to critically assess our traditions and remove questionable parts, yet maintain distinctive elements. Thus Scripture provides the grand narrative of history because it is its only divine interpretation.

As missionaries, we enter the foreign lands with Scripture in hand. Through the language and thought of the indigenous people, we display the beauty of God's grace. We show this grace through the inscripturated revelation as the divine narrative, which translates the world, and we thus show the culture which

we are reaching how they fit within that history of redemption…
in equality with ours. This allows each culture to keep its
identity intact, accounts for the necessity of community for the
realization of truth, and ties the global church together as one
eclectic unity.

END NOTES

1. Patrick Stefan is from the United States, and a second
   year M.Div. student at Reformed Theological Seminary,
   Washington DC Campus. He is currently a Student of
   Theology under care of the Reformed Presbyterian Church
   of North America.

2. Jean-Francois Lyotard, *The Postmodern Condition: A Report
   on Knowledge*, trans. G. Bennington and B. Massumi
   (French Original, 1979; Minneapolis: University of
   Minnesota Press, 1984), xxiv.

3. John Calvin *The Institutes of the Christian Religion* vol 1 ed.
   John T. McNeill (Westminster John Knox Press, Louisville,
   KY, 2006) pg 159-160.

4. Wilbert R. Shenk *Changing Frontiers of Mission*.
   (Maryknoll, NY: Orbis Books, 1999) pg 164.

BIBLIOGRAPHY

Calvin, John. *The Institutes of the Christian Religion* vol 1 ed.
   John T. McNeill Westminster John Knox Press, Louisville,
   KY, 2006.

Grenz, Stanley J. *A Primer on Postmodernism*. Grand Rapids,
   MI: Eerdmans, 1996.

Penner, Myron B. ed. *Christianity and the Postmodern Turn.* Grand Rapids, MI: Brazos Press, 2006.

Ricoeur, Paul. *Interpretation Theory: Discourse and the Surplus of Meaning.* Fort Worth, TX: The Texas Christian University Press, 1976.

Shenk, Wilbert R. *Changing Frontiers of Mission.* Maryknoll, NY: Orbis Books, 1999.

Smith, James K.A. *Who's Afraid of Postmodernism?: Taking Derrida, Lyotard, and Foucault to Church.* Grand Rapids, MI: Baker Academic, 2006.

Lightning Source UK Ltd.
Milton Keynes UK
28 May 2010

154842UK00001B/47/P

9 780865 850125